ROUTLEDGE LIBRARY EDITIONS: FAMILY

Volume 15

SOCIAL WORK WITH FAMILIES

SOCIAL WORK WITH FAMILIES

Perceptions of Social Casework Among Clients of a Family Service Unit

ERIC SAINSBURY

LONDON AND NEW YORK

First published in 1975 by Routledge & Kegan Paul Ltd

This edition first published in 2023
by Routledge
4 Park Square, Milton Park, Abingdon, Oxon OX14 4RN

and by Routledge
605 Third Avenue, New York, NY 10158

Routledge is an imprint of the Taylor & Francis Group, an informa business

© 1975 Eric Sainsbury

All rights reserved. No part of this book may be reprinted or reproduced or utilised in any form or by any electronic, mechanical, or other means, now known or hereafter invented, including photocopying and recording, or in any information storage or retrieval system, without permission in writing from the publishers.

Trademark notice: Product or corporate names may be trademarks or registered trademarks, and are used only for identification and explanation without intent to infringe.

British Library Cataloguing in Publication Data
A catalogue record for this book is available from the British Library

ISBN: 978-1-032-51072-9 (Set)
ISBN: 978-1-032-53370-4 (Volume 15) (hbk)
ISBN: 978-1-032-53375-9 (Volume 15) (pbk)
ISBN: 978-1-003-41172-7 (Volume 15) (ebk)

DOI: 10.4324/9781003411727

Publisher's Note
The publisher has gone to great lengths to ensure the quality of this reprint but points out that some imperfections in the original copies may be apparent.

Disclaimer
The publisher has made every effort to trace copyright holders and would welcome correspondence from those they have been unable to trace.

Social Work with Families

Perceptions of social casework
among clients of a Family
Service Unit

Eric Sainsbury

*Department of Sociological Studies,
University of Sheffield*

LONDON AND BOSTON
ROUTLEDGE & KEGAN PAUL

First published in 1975
by Routledge & Kegan Paul Ltd
Broadway House, 68-74 Carter Lane,
London EC4V 5EL and
9 Park Street,
Boston, Mass. 02108, USA
Set in Linotype 10/11 pt Pilgrim
and printed in Great Britain by
Northumberland Press Ltd, Gateshead
© Eric Sainsbury 1975
No part of this book may be reproduced in
any form without permission from the
publisher, except for the quotation of brief
passages in criticism
ISBN 0 7100 8039 5 (c)
     0 7100 8040 9 (p)

for Audrey

Contents

		page
	General editor's introduction	xi
	Acknowledgments	xiii
1	The origins of the study	1
	The study	3
2	Meeting the families	7
	Sub-groupings within the twenty-seven families	8
	National and local comparisons	10
	Comparative findings	11
	Approaching the families	14
3	Referral, intake and help at the point of crisis	17
	Introduction	17
	Referral agents	18
	The extent and consistency of other sources of help	21
	The families' own efforts in coping	25
	Referral needs and the relevance of immediate help	26
	Relating help to need	28
	The influences exerted on clients' perceptions of the helpfulness of services	32
4	Continuing help	38
	The scope of help offered and the subjects discussed	39
	Professional help and help through friendship	49
	The most helpful form of help	55

CONTENTS

5	Memories of the duration of contact in relation to the families' preferences for particular social workers	64
	Families' preferences for particular social workers, and their reasons	67
6	Relationships between families and social workers	71
	The clients' feelings for their most recent social workers	73
	The use made of the social workers' personal disclosures	77
	The use of authority and the setting of limits	79
	The clients' descriptions of the attitudes of their preferred social workers	86
	A comment on worker-client relationships in terms of role-behaviour	89
7	Changes in the families' lives	94
	The findings for sub-groupings	98
8	'Good' and 'successful' work	103
	The place of ethical factors	103
	Befriending and social functioning	104
	The relationship between 'good' and 'successful'	105
	The Committee interview	108
9	Summary, conclusions and suggestions	112
	A summary of findings	113
	Consequential hypotheses about the practice of family casework	119
	Some factors which may indicate or lead to success	121
	Appendix I Outline of guided interviews with the families	127
	II Schedule for interviews with the social workers	129
	III The families interviewed	133
	IV Major subjects discussed in interviews	134
	V Recollections of the length of contact	138
	VI Selected transcriptions from the interviews with families	141
	Bibliography	169
	Index	171

Tables

1	National and local comparisons	12
2	Routes of referral for the twenty-seven families	19
3	The availability of other 'helpers'	23
4	Referral needs	27
5	Need and help	30
6	The categories and scope of help	40
7	The subjects most frequently discussed	48
8	The most helpful form of help	56
9	Families who have referred other families	57
10	A comparison of workers' and families' perceptions of the most effective help	59
11	Perceived changes in social functioning (1)	61
12	Recollections of the length of contact (summary)	65
13	The sequential position of the preferred worker	66
14	Reasons for clients' preferences	69
15	Clients' feelings for the most recent social workers	75
16	Firmness and limits employed by the social workers, and the families' responses to them	82
17	The importance ascribed to attitudes in the relationships of social workers	90
18	Perceived changes in social functioning (2)	96
19	Frequency of change in the factors of social functioning	97

General editor's introduction

The Library of Social Work was originally designed to make a contribution to the recent significant expansion in social work education. Not only were increasing numbers of students training for social work, but the changing demands of the work and widening view of its theoretical bases were producing considerable changes in the basic curriculum of social work education. In this situation a library of short texts intended to introduce a subject, to assess its relevance for social work, and to guide further reading had a distinctive contribution to make. The continuing success of the Library of Social Work shows that this contribution is still highly valued.

The Library of Social Work will, therefore, continue to produce short introductory texts, but it will also enlarge its range to include the longer, more sustained treatment of subjects relevant to social work. Monographs reporting research, collections of papers, the more detailed and substantial explanation of the knowledge base of social work, could all be encompassed within this wider definition of the scope of the Library of Social Work.

This monograph presents the results of a research project into the perceptions of social casework among clients of a Family Service Unit. The opinions of their social workers are also presented. The author suggests that the study represents a modest exercise, and it must be acknowledged that the number of families studied is quite small—twenty-seven. We should, however, see the study as a significant contribution to a major present preoccupation in social work. As Pinker (quoted in this book) has said, clients are citizens (this in itself is an interesting revival of an idea close to the heart of Charles Loch much earlier in this century) who use the social services. Our ignorance of their perspective on these services is massive: 'We know almost nothing about the reasons for which citizens use services, as they do, or about what attitudes lead to them feeling deterred or encouraged in the search for assistance.' This study develops our understanding of the clients and of their social workers in the context of an agency usually considered to be dealing with people below average in intelligence. Yet, as Eric Sainsbury concluded, 'Their experiences have been my main concern, and I was impressed by and grateful for the clarity with which they described them.' This book should be an encouragement to those who believe that clients can be approached and asked about their experiences with beneficial and encouraging results.

There are a number of findings in this study which are of interest in themselves and suggest fruitful hypotheses for future research. For example, it seems that 'no special advantage in the quality of relationship or outcome of work accrues from avoiding changes of worker'. 'When clients invest feelings in their relationship with workers, these are perceived as ends in themselves, irrespective of needs and problems.' The client's awareness of the worker's empathy is 'assisted by the worker's appropriate disclosures about his own life'. These and other statements question our received wisdom and it is good that they do. As we study client–social worker interaction and formulate more sharply our questions and observations we shall gradually gain a hold on an elusive complex of problems that at present bewilder and baffle us. This book is one contribution to this patient process.

Acknowledgments

This study would not have been possible without the co-operation of twenty-seven families and eleven social workers. They gave their help generously and with great kindness and trust, and I wish to express my gratitude to them all.

The study was undertaken during an eight months' period in 1972-3. Deborah Page worked closely with me, and I am considerably indebted to her, both as a stimulating and delightful colleague, and for the particular responsibility she took in the national survey, the selection of families and the records-search. Because of her help and her discretion, it was possible to conduct all the interviews without preconceptions about the families, their circumstances and their problems. The Department of Health and Social Security provided financial support for the study, and have very kindly consented to the preparation of the present book from the report submitted to them in April 1973. I wish to record my gratitude to several members of that Department for their interest in my earlier proposal and for the enjoyable discussions we have had since then. Similarly, I have been fortunate in the encouragement, guidance and friendship of members of the Family Service Units, particularly Felicity Craven, Rex Halliwell and Norman Proctor. With Rex Halliwell's help, Deborah Page and I were able to secure the co-operation of the members of all nineteen FSUs in completing our national questionnaire. My thanks to the ninety-five social workers who did so, and who tolerated the problems of definition which it posed.

Anne Graham undertook much of the typing of the original research report and all the labour involved in preparing the present book for publication. I am grateful to her not only for the speed and reliability of her work but for the good humour with which she has confronted the most disheartening piles of script. My best thanks are due to my wife for unfailing encouragement at all stages of the work; and to her and to Juliet Berry for their patience in helping me to check typescript and proofs.

ACKNOWLEDGMENTS

Many other people have discussed the project, given advice, and in various other ways supported my efforts: I think particularly of Jackie Burgoyne, Liz Dodds, Cissie Goldberg, Felicity Jackson and Tim Robinson for their advice and of Christine Gandy for her substantial administrative and secretarial support, particularly in the first phase of the research. My thanks to them all.

Author's note

All names used in the study are fictitious, and considerable efforts have been made to maintain total anonymity in the case material. Where details have been altered, however, the changes do not in any way affect the validity of the material as it is used in the study.

1
The origins of the study

This book presents the opinions and experiences of twenty-seven families who have received help from the Sheffield Family Service Unit. This is how they described social work and social workers from one agency. The opinions of their social workers are also presented, so as to compare how the helping process looks from both ends.

If considered in isolation, this modest exercise may seem a trivial one. It represents, however, a small addition to the studies of clients' perceptions of social work, particularly those carried out by Butrym (1968), Goldberg (1970), Mayer and Timms (1970), Timms (1973), and McKay and others (1973); it relates to the work of a different agency and to the experiences of families who, it is reasonable to infer, are representative of those known to Family Service Units throughout the country.

My concern has also been to introduce some considerations which may help towards identifying criteria of success in social work practice, and thus towards the definition of purpose. Much of the study deals with what clients identify as good practice and appropriate personal qualities among social workers. As Mayer and Timms have pointed out, although the appraisals made by clients are not the only considerations in shaping services, effective service requires us to know something about the responses and reactions of those we seek to help. Similarly, purposefulness in professional practice cannot be defined without regard for how it is perceived by those for whose benefit practice is formulated. Mullen and Dumpson (1972) have written, 'Many projects fail to reach their goals because the following question has been inadequately considered: on what basis and towards what end will who do what to whom, for how long, with what effect, at what cost, and with what benefits?' Some statement of purpose is essential if evaluative studies of social work practice are to have any meaning, and it is important for this statement to be made with reference to the views of those directly engaged in practice, as clients or as social workers. The morale of both depends on their having some ideas about what it is all for, and on their convictions that the purpose is not a remote one but is related to their actual experiences of working together. Yet the purpose of social work is at present customarily identified in one of three ways at various removes from these experiences: by reference to a high-level generalization of moral or ethical intention properly reserved for speech-days and annual reports; by reference to the functions of social agencies, which, while they save the words 'success' and 'outcome' from vacuity, may take on the look of bureaucratic definitions whose only justification is to keep the organization running; or by reference to conceptual and analytical frameworks borrowed from political, sociological, psychiatric or psychological theorists who have neither been clients nor had the social worker's experience of trying to help them. A more satisfactory approach to the identifying of purpose may lie in a consideration of the processes intrinsic to practice and of the ways in which clients, social workers, agency administrators and policy-makers (and others standing in various relationships to the needs and problems with which people seek help) perceive what takes place in social work and variously assess it. I do not suggest or believe that a single definition of purpose will be found: emphasis on consensus of purpose would probably lead back to those high levels of generalization where no practical illumination and guidance is available. It is no doubt true of 'purpose' and of 'success' that different kinds of work-situations need different criteria. But by identifying and comparing different views of purpose and success, the practitioner can better clarify his own aims and the appropriate style of his day-to-day work. Social workers are sometimes accused of regarding their work as so vital that they do not have time to evaluate it. Their critics both look for and profess to find this conceit. An alternative explanation which more adequately fits the experience of many social workers is that they keep excessively busy as a defence against the despair or cynicism bred by trying to define a sense of purpose and achievement from the conflicting theories of social scientists and the shifting and increasing demands of administrators and politicians.

Little help is available from within the profession of social work, where justifications of practice tend to rely on broad and undifferentiated descriptions (such as 'problem solving') or on elaborate definitions of techniques, and where there are as yet few strategic models for practice or few, if any, theories which are comprehensive and yet precise. Spencer (1970) has written that

THE ORIGINS OF THE STUDY

'the organizational problem for the social worker is not simply being a professional in a bureaucracy; it is the problem of uncertainty about the nature of social work'.

Similarly, from the client's point of view, Pinker (1971) has written, 'We know almost nothing about the reasons for which citizens use services as they do, or about what attitudes lead them to feel deterred or encouraged in the search for assistance.'

In the present study, therefore, an attempt is made to discover some of these feelings and experiences among the clients of one social service, and to offer some indications about purpose in social work by asking clients, social workers and policy-makers what they think constitutes good work and successful work. No theories will be imported as arbiters of 'good' and 'successful'. The opinions of the clients are given equal weight with the views of the professionals, and I have assumed the honesty of all respondents equally. As far as possible, I have tried to avoid interpreting clients' statements and fitting them into professional or ideological models. This study risks naïveté, therefore, in order to avoid those psychotherapeutic or ideological games which aim 'to resolve the problems of the amateur according to the rules of the professional'. In studying the work of the Sheffield FSU, I have found no instance of clients being expected to learn such rules. Some examples will, however, be given of clients' apparent identification with the value-orientations of their social workers. As we shall see, the extent to which, and the ways in which, such an identification relates to notions of 'good' and 'successful' work are matters of great complexity; they will be touched upon, but merit more study than they have hitherto received.

The study

The Family Service Units are voluntary family casework agencies. Established in 1948 on the pioneer work of the war-time Pacifist Service Units, they have been associated from the start with 'problem families'—a label which has been variously worded, but which has always been associated with that small group of families who, because of the multiplicity and intractability of their problems and needs, are thought to require more intensive and comprehensive help over long periods than the statutory services consider themselves able to offer. The problems and needs presented by families referred to the FSU are usually multiple, interacting, and rooted in poverty, physical or mental incapacity, inter-personal strife, or overwhelming emotional stress. The history and work of the Units are described by Stephens (1945), Philp and Timms (1957), Philp (1963), and Goldring (1973).

THE ORIGINS OF THE STUDY

In the present study, twenty-seven families have been asked what their difficulties were at the time of their referral to the Sheffield Unit, and what help and attitudes they expected to find there. They have been invited to identify the characteristics of their favourite social worker, to describe the help they have received from the Unit and to pick out the most helpful form of help. From the answers to these questions it has been possible to learn something about the clients' feelings at the time of referral, their relationships with other 'helpers' at that time, and the content of their memories of the processes of casework. Similarly, their most recent social workers have been asked to recall the reasons for referral, to identify the favourite and most successful social worker(s) in each case, and to express an opinion (and to guess their clients' opinions) about the most helpful kinds of help offered. They were also invited to review the changes that have taken place in the lives of their clients during the period of contact. Their memories of events have been compared with the memories of their clients; and every aspect of the study has been checked as far as possible against the day-to-day records of the agency.

The burdens the study placed on the generosity, patience, honesty, good humour, tolerance and trust of families and social workers alike have been heavy. Enjoyment in meeting them is accompanied by my gratitude for the practical insights they gave.

All interviews with clients were tape-recorded. Interviews were conducted with 'families', rather than with pre-determined members of the families. This may appear to be methodologically unsatisfactory; but other choices would have been more so in relation to the information required. Most FSU work is contained within the workers' visits to the homes of their clients. In this study, the families were visited at home and seen in much the same way as the social workers see them: sometimes the children stayed in the room, sometimes they were sent out to play; husbands (whether or not by legal marriage) were usually present, but where they were not the situation in each case accurately re-created the customary setting of the social worker's visits. Visits were arranged to suit the convenience of the families, so that no member was excluded who wished to be present or who would normally be present for an interview with the Unit worker. Interviewing in a grouping familiar to the respondents may have provided advantages of spontaneity and reduced a little the artificiality of the study-situation.

All interviews with all respondents were conducted by the writer. The interviews with the families were guided, but without a formal questionnaire. The outline used for these interviews is set out as Appendix I.

THE ORIGINS OF THE STUDY

Interviews with the social workers were not tape-recorded. A copy of the schedule used appears as Appendix II.

The interview with the policy-makers was conducted as a group interview, annexed to an ordinary business meeting of the Committee. It was decided to proceed in this way, rather than by individual interviews with Committee members, because of the number of new variables which would have been introduced: occupation and training, the extent of social work knowledge and experience, the various influences which might lead members to say different things in private interviews and in Committee meetings, the unknown extent to which individual members contribute to joint discussions of the Unit's policy, or influence the practice of individual social workers outside the Committee meetings. It is doubtful whether much use could have been made of all the information that would have been derived from individual interviews. Members were treated, therefore, as a committee rather than as individuals. Presumably, the final range of conclusions and views expressed in the group was acceptable to the members, and represented, broadly speaking, the influences they exerted on their employees.

Finally, mention should be made of some matters which I hoped to consider in addition to the main areas of factual information and opinion. First, it is usually assumed that the clients of Family Service Units are of below average intelligence; I wondered, therefore, whether the families would find difficulty in achieving enough verbal precision to answer questions relating to their preferences for particular helpers or modes of help, and whether concentration would present problems. Few difficulties were experienced. Once the guided interview started (that is to say, after some introductions and getting used to the tape-recorder) concentration was usually considerable; interruptions were not tolerated, neighbours were introduced and sent away, children were packed off if troublesome. Some respondents effectively made their contributions in as little as half an hour; with most, the time taken was three-quarters to one hour. Even when interviews were longer than this, concentration rarely flagged, and in only two cases did respondents lose the thread in their comments. For the rest, provided enough time was allowed, the respondents themselves brought any straying thoughts back to the subject in hand. In the matter of verbal precision, time was again important, together with some prompting of the 'I'm-not-sure-that-I've-quite-got-it-yet' kind. One respondent, for example, who felt particularly strong respect and admiration for a social worker's moral goodness, found it hard to get beyond describing him as 'smashing', and some time was necessary to discard irrelevant meanings and to emphasize the intended ones; but she achieved

5

precision by her own efforts. But, as she said in conclusion, when we had boiled it all down, he *was* a 'smashing feller'.

Second, FSU families are usually thought to live lives of considerable deprivation, recurrent crises and uncertainty, from which long-term aspirations and achievements are absent. Would moral chaos also be part of this situation? The interviews showed the presence of a higher regard for values—particularly in relationships—than the social workers often realized; in many families there was also an apparent acceptance that, however great the stress and unpredictability of life within the family, order and structure are desirable, and the feeling that, if structure is imposed within the context of certain kinds of relationships, it is not resented in the long run, though it almost certainly is at the time. It seemed that this was not simply the sign of a need for emotional security. The comments of several clients related to ethical or moral value, and it proved difficult to separate their regard for moral and ethical aspects of helping from their regard for material and emotional help. This matter merits further study than it will receive here; it may be as important in the debate about purpose in social work as the more usual considerations of welfare provision and emotional and attitudinal change.

In order to avoid complexity in the presentation of the study, notes about theoretical considerations or the findings from other studies are annexed to the end of each chapter.

Notes

In relation to the applicability of psychotherapeutic models to social work practice, mention should be made of the studies of the *means* of help undertaken by associates of Carl Rogers, which achieve far greater relevance to the problems of social workers in certain case situations than do more global statements of the purposes of help. Variables in the therapist are studied by Truax and Carkhuff (1967) and Carkhuff and Berenson (1967), together with studies of the negative as well as the positive effects of psychotherapeutic relationships. Their findings are relevant to those of the present study in respect of the personal characteristics of the social workers most liked by the families.

2
Meeting the families

The intention of the project was to interview thirty families who had been in touch with the Sheffield Unit for not less than one-and-a-half years and not more than three-and-a-half. The purpose of these limits, worked out in consultation with the social workers, was to exclude those families who might still be in the crises of their referral situation—where resources had not yet been adequately mobilized, or where relationships with the social agencies were unstable or uncertain—and to exclude also those families with whom social work may have settled into a wholly undynamic friendliness. Originally, the families were to be selected from the Unit's list of closed cases; but it became apparent from the intake statistics that the limits of selection would have made it necessary to include families with whom work had started more than ten years before the project. It was considered that memories might be very unreliable after so long a period.

The project sample was therefore made up of fifteen families from the closed cases list and fifteen from the open cases, thus providing two groups for certain comparisons. The criteria for selection were as follows:

> work with 'closed case' families should have ended within three years of the start of the project (June 1972);
> all families should have been in contact with the Unit within the time-limits set out earlier; and re-opened cases should be excluded, save where the total of all periods of contact fell within the time-limits;
> all families should live in the city of Sheffield (at the time of the study, 25 per cent of the Unit's intake was from Derbyshire);
> finding and visiting should not risk any serious hardship for any family; this excluded, for example, families thought to be

'on the run';

the most recent social worker should not have been a student.

From the closed cases list, these criteria produced fourteen families, but, as three could not be traced and two refused to be interviewed, only nine remained. From the open cases list, fifteen families met the criteria; one family refused to be interviewed and was therefore replaced by another who met the criteria except for very brief contact with the Unit seven years before the current referral.

Because of the shortage of families within the criteria, the trial interviews (to acclimatize the interviewer and to test the interview guidelines) were conducted with three families whose acquaintance with the Unit fell outside the time-limits but who satisfied other criteria. As it was not necessary to change the methods or content of interviews between the trial interviews and the rest of the study, and as the numbers available were small, the ideas and viewpoints of these families are included. Reference will be made later to any distinctive qualities in the replies of this sub-group of longer-term clients. So that they may be identified throughout this report, however, it is appropriate to name them at this stage: Harris (open case), 5 years 11 months at the time of interview; Norris (open case), 5 years 5 months; Sanders (closed case), 5 years 5 months.

Thus, the study is concerned with ten closed cases and seventeen open cases: twenty-seven families in all. In view of the difficulty in finding enough families for the study, sampling techniques were not required and the matching of sub-groups was not possible. The families form a population, rather than a sample; they provide a comprehensive view of the Sheffield Unit's modes of work other than with recently referred families or those in very long-term friendly contact. From so small a population of families it would be inappropriate to make generalizations about the clients of other agencies or, indeed, of other Units. It has proved possible, however, to formulate some hypotheses, and to establish how far the families interviewed may be considered as representative of other families currently in touch with the Sheffield Unit and with other Family Service Units.

Sub-groupings within the twenty-seven families

This study is very largely concerned with the ways in which clients perceive the intervention of social workers. In discussion with the social workers, seven factors were defined which it was thought might significantly influence perceptions. The presentation of findings is partly related, therefore, to a discussion of these factors;

and they will be employed also as criteria for sub-groupings among the replies received. The seven factors are set out below and examined in the following paragraphs:

(1) the problems at the time of referral;
(2) 'single parent' or 'whole' families;
(3) differences in referral agents or initiators of contact;
(4) the availability of other helpers at the time of referral;
(5) the length of contact with the Unit;
(6) the number of changes of social workers during the contact;
(7) whether the experience of social work was continuing or had ended at the time of interview (open or closed cases).

In this study, problems at the time of referral are described principally in accordance with the families' own accounts; comparisons are drawn with the accounts offered by the social workers; and the families' needs are related to the help offered to them. For the purposes of comparison with families known to other Units, a classification of referral problems is also employed, based wholly on the social workers' views. But the isolation of single factors, which such a classification requires, is an unreliable and distorting process, and this form of classification is not used otherwise than for the comparisons made in this chapter.

Among the twenty-seven families, five were single-parent families (all mothers coping alone). We shall consider whether the social worker's relationship is, in some way, closer with a single-parent family than with others, and whether the single parents' perceptions of the relationship or of the outcome of casework are different in any way.

An attempt will be made to relate, so far as the numbers permit, the referral agents to the clients' preliminary expectations of the Unit and its services. The availability of other helpers at the time of referral presented difficulties of data collection; records varied in completeness and reliability, and the memories of clients and workers were sometimes too uncertain (by their own admission) to draw out reliable sub-groupings of families. It has been possible, however, to make some general comments about the availability of help to families at the time of referral, and in particular about the quality of their relationships with other helpers.

Reference has already been made to the fifth and seventh factors —sub-groupings of those in very long-term contact, and of open and closed cases.

The number of Unit workers in touch with any one family during the whole period of social work intervention varied from one to five, to which a variable number of students may be added. It was thought that a family's perception of the casework relationship—and, indeed, the nature of that relationship—might change according to the number of workers involved. Numbers were too small to achieve a comprehensive analysis, but this matter has been studied in two respects: first, in relation to the clients' expressed preferences for particular workers, and second, in respect of worker-client relationships in the four cases where only one social worker had been in touch with the family.

National and local comparisons

In order to establish how far the families might be regarded as representative of others known to the Sheffield and other Units, and thus to indicate how far the study might have some national rather than merely local relevance, a letter and questionnaire were sent out, with the assistance of FSU Headquarters, to social workers in all Units, including Sheffield. Each FSU worker completed a questionnaire covering his total workload, and Unit Organizers were asked to ensure the inclusion of all current work and the avoidance of duplicate entries. All nineteen Units agreed to take part, and ninety-five out of ninety-six social workers returned completed questionnaires. It is likely that the national figures represent an underestimate of the total caseload, partly because of the missing questionnaire and partly because of two anomalies in the returns: one Unit excluded families currently being visited by students; another included casual contacts not normally included in the caseload returns.

The criteria chosen to reflect the characteristics of families using FSU services were:

(1) the number of children, including those normally living at home and those in care, but excluding those who have grown up and left home; families with ten or more children were grouped together;
(2) the extent of special schooling: this category was sub-divided into (i) schools for ESN children and (ii) other special schools, including those for the severely subnormal; this distinction was drawn in order to reflect the closer association, generally believed to exist, with the home environment of mild sub-normality than of other handicaps. However, this second sub-division, in order to avoid too much categorization, included open-air schools and ex-approved schools;
(3) the employment or unemployment of the father—that is, of the husband or cohabitee normally living in the household; as the study was undertaken at a time of high unemployment,

MEETING THE FAMILIES

a father was considered unemployed only if he had been out of work for three months;
(4) the absence of the father, husband or cohabitee;
(5) the family's social class, as assessed by the father's present or last occupation; unfortunately, a few workers applied a class definition to all families irrespective of the presence of a father; some others failed to record the work of all fathers; but in spite of errors in interpretation, the figures give an indication of the spread of social class;
(6) serious debts, defined as serious by their consequences rather than by their size; for example, a family was judged to be in serious debt if on the point of eviction for unpaid rent, if their gas or electricity had been disconnected, or if a parent was on the point of (or actually experiencing) imprisonment for unpaid fines, debts or maintenance orders;
(7) one parent appearing as defendant in a Criminal Court during the previous twelve months, or being currently the subject of an order or sentence of a Criminal Court;
(8) the social workers' opinions of the primary problem at the time of referral; respondents chose one of six categories of problem, to reflect their views of where help was most essential at the start of the case.

The information from the study of the twenty-seven families refers, for those currently in contact with the Unit, to the period January–March 1973; for closed cases (bearing in mind that the national comparisons were concerned only with current cases), information was drawn from a time twelve months before the closure of each case, in order to avoid the extreme situations which might obtain at times of referral or of closure, when debts, for example, would probably be respectively much higher or much lower than for the average open case. It was hoped that information from twelve months preceding closure could be regarded as more comparable with the cross-section of 'stages of progress' which a study of open cases provides.

Comparative findings

There are nineteen FSUs in the United Kingdom, employing ninety-six social workers of whom ninety-five responded to the questionnaire. Units employ from three to ten social workers; the average for each Unit is five.

TABLE 1 *National and local comparisons*

	National	Sheffield	Present study
Total number of families	1064	85	27
Total number of children	4471	366	109
Average number of children in each family	4.2	4.3	4.0
No. and % of families having the following number of children	(%)	(%)	(%)*
0	5 (0.5)	1 (1.2)	1 (3.7)
1	68 (6.4)	8 (9.2)	0
2	149 (14.0)	11 (13.0)	3 (11.1)
3	194 (18.2)	11 (13.0)	7 (25.9)
4	211 (19.8)	15 (17.6)	9 (33.3)
5	175 (16.4)	16 (18.8)	0
6	117 (11.0)	6 (7.1)	1 (3.7)
7	64 (6.0)	8 (9.2)	3 (11.1)
8	34 (3.2)	4 (4.7)	1 (3.7)
9	20 (1.9)	1 (1.2)	0
10 (+)	25 (2.3)	3 (3.5)	2 (7.4)
Not known	2	1	
No. and % of children in special schools for subnormal	240 (5.4)	16 (4.8)	3 (2.8)
No. and % in other special schools	116 (2.6)	8 (2.4)	3 (2.8)
No. and % of families where father is employed now or in last 3 months	380 (35.7)	26 (31)	8 (29.6)
No. and % of families with father unemployed for at least 3 months	391 (36.8)	46 (54)	14 (51.8)
No. and % of families without fathers at home	290 (27.3)	13 (15)	5 (24.1)
Not known	3		
No. of fathers whose present/last employment falls into the following categories			
white collar	15 (1.4)	1 (1.2)	0

*Percentages are included, although their value is limited for so small a number.

	National		Sheffield		Present study	
		(%)		(%)		(%)
skilled	62	(5.8)	7	(8.2)	3	(11.1)
semi-skilled	175	(16.4)	10	(11.8)	4	(14.8)
unskilled	463	(43.5)	54	(63.5)	14	(51.8)
not known/not applicable	349	(32.8)	13	(15.3)	6	(22.2)

By redistributing the 'not known/not applicable' category proportionately to other categories—in order to indicate the spread of social class in terms of employment potential—the percentages are as follows:

white collar	2.0	1.8	—
skilled	8.7	12.7	14.3
semi-skilled	24.5	17.3	19.0
unskilled	64.8	68.2	66.7

No. of families with serious debts	482 (45.3)	45 (53)	12*(44.4)
No. of families where parents have been in Criminal Courts during previous 12 months and/or are subject to Court orders at present	208 (19.5)	36 (42)	12 (44.4)
No. of families referred for each of the following reasons			
financial and/or accommodation	321 (30.0)	29 (34.0)	8 (29.6)
disturbed family relations	334 (31.4)	20 (24.0)	8 (29.6)
inadequate care of children	136 (12.8)	13 (15.0)	4 (14.8)
major personality/character disorder	122 (11.5)	10 (12.0)	3 (11.2)
serious anxiety/distress	122 (11.5)	12 (14.0)	4 (14.8)
physical ill health	21 (2.0)	1 (1.0)	0
Not known	8 (0.8)	0	0

(6 workers and one Unit organizer commented on the difficulty or inadequacy of these categories)

---

* Possible underestimate: records do not always register Administration Orders.

National and local comparisons are given in Table 1. As can be seen, the statistics from the Study families closely approximate, in proportional terms, to those from Family Service Unit families as a whole, both nationally and in the Sheffield service. The average number of children in an FSU family is 4·2 (compared with 2·4 in the general population); the percentage of children in ESN schools is 5·4 (general percentage is 0·7); the percentage in other special schools is 2·6 (2·8 in the present study; 1·0 in the general statistics); unemployment, serious debts and Criminal Court appearances all run at high levels in all Units and in the present study. In general, it is reasonable to assume that the families interviewed in the study are typical of families known to Family Service Units throughout the country in that they share in approximately the same proportions the characteristics defined at the start of this section. (A more detailed study of differences between the returns from local Units has been published elsewhere, and information can be obtained from the author or from National FSU, London.)

Approaching the families

The procedure employed in meeting each family was as follows:

The current or most recent social worker visited the family to talk about the study and, if possible, to obtain permission to bring the interviewer to meet them. The social workers were asked to explain to the families that

(1) the researcher (E.S.) is a friend of the Unit who works at the University and who would like to meet them to hear about their experiences with social workers and how social workers behave towards them; the words 'research' and 'researcher' were not to be used;

(2) E.S. does not work for the Unit or at Unit House, but he helps to train social workers; he wants to visit some families to see whether more could be done to help social workers to be more helpful;

(3) no information would be passed on to the Unit or any other social workers, and their names would not be mentioned anywhere.

If the family at this point agreed to allow E.S. to visit, the worker informed them that

(4) he would be bringing a tape-recorder to record the conversation, instead of making notes in a notebook; but the tape would not be heard by anybody from the Unit, the Town Hall, etc.

If the family was still willing to meet him,

(5) a time convenient for all the family was to be arranged, when the social worker could introduce E.S.; the social worker would leave as soon as the introduction was made.

As has been noted earlier, three families refused to be visited.

When the social worker introduced the interviewer to the family and left him with them, the interviewer explained again the points set out in 1-4 above, and again asked the family if they would be willing to help. If the family showed any hesitation, the interviewer suggested an unrecorded discussion about the sorts of subjects he would be interested to hear about. At the end of this, the interviewer left and a further appointment was made, subject to the family's willingness. Initial hesitation was shown by three families, and this procedure was followed; all three agreed to be interviewed on the second visit.

It had been the interviewer's expectation that up to three visits would be necessary before families agreed to a recorded interview. This was not the case. The interview was accepted without hesitation by twenty-four families and positively welcomed by many; a sense of occasion was present during several interviews. The interviews became well-known among clients meeting in the clothing store, play group and Mothers' Group, and some clients not included in the list for interviewing complained to their caseworkers. The caseworkers picked up no hint of regret from the families interviewed. It seems likely that some responses may have been coloured by positive feelings generated in this exercise; a later note has been made of this possibility, especially in relation to the question to respondents whether they felt they could speak their minds honestly to the caseworkers.

Many families had experience of the use of tape-recorders among their friends and relatives; embarrassment rarely lasted more than a few minutes.

At the start of the interview, there was a brief discussion of the kinds of questions which would be asked, and a request to families not to try to answer any questions they disliked. (This problem did not arise.) With their permission, the recorder was then switched on. When young children were present, the family acclimatized to the recorder by allowing the children to play with it—to record nursery rhymes, songs, school dinner menus, etc. These were played back and the guided interview was started. At the end of the interview, respondents were asked if they wished to hear all or part of it re-played. Many did, but more for the amusement of hearing themselves than to check the content of their replies. The recorder was then switched off and disconnected. Usually the interview continued as an informal discussion for some time afterwards, mostly on the subject of the interview; this was often an interesting and profitable discussion, but the recorder was not switched on again.

The introduction by the social workers of the idea of the study eased the interviewer's approach to the families very considerably. As has been noted, most families were willing to be interviewed; in only four families was mistrust openly apparent during interviews, and of these only two remained obviously mistrustful throughout. The method of approach to the families may well have coloured the tone of their responses to questions; but it may equally well have heightened their willingness to speak honestly.

Husband and wife (or cohabitees) were interviewed together in seventeen cases. Five wives were widowed, divorced or separated from their husbands, and three others were interviewed alone because of the husband's absence at work or in prison. In only two families did the husbands decline to be interviewed. Children were present during the interviews with fifteen families, and often took an active part.

3
Referral, intake and help at the point of crisis

Introduction

E. M. Goldberg (1970) has related the satisfaction of clients to the meeting of both material and emotional needs within a single process of help. This theme will run through many aspects of the present discussion; for example, I shall suggest that material and other forms of help are sometimes linked emotionally, especially in a crisis situation when one form of help may symbolize the other. Similarly, by comparing the kinds of help made available to families with their recollections of the main areas of discussion during interviews, it will be suggested that help relating to financial and material problems was often accompanied by an emphasis, in the concern of both workers and clients, upon the feelings and emotional needs of the wives and mothers. (In a study of FSU work, Jackson (1973) has similarly demonstrated the co-existence of material and emotional problems, and has emphasized the need for concurrent help in both areas.)

The replies received from the families suggest, however, that the availability of relevant help does not in itself ensure the client's satisfaction. Mayer and Timms (1970) have drawn attention to the influence of clients' expectations, beliefs and feelings at the time of referral upon their perceptions both of the social workers and of the help subsequently offered. Overton (1960) has suggested further that the client's perceptions of the personality of the social worker are more influential on his attitudes than his expectations or perceptions of the agency. These opinions, taken together, suggest that the effectiveness of a social service is judged by its users more in terms of the perceived personalities of social workers than by any official statement or advertisement of the agency's work; and that the functions of an agency are less influential on consumer-opinion than are the processes of perception taking place between users and staff.

The following pages, therefore, are concerned not with the official functions of the FSU and the relevance of these to the families' requests for help, but with the more personal expectations (of social work help and the attitudes of social workers) which the clients brought with them. These expectations will be related to the broad spectrum of 'helpers' available to the families at the time of referral, and to the relationship between need and help in the first two weeks of contact. An attempt will be made to convey the emotional climate in which the social work was practised as a possible influence upon a family's acceptance of the social worker, particularly at times when uncertain, equivocal or hostile relationships with other potential helpers (formal and informal) had intensified the panic or sense of isolation which sometimes accompany the experience of material or emotional need. It will be shown that in some families—even after years of contact with other social workers and an accumulation of favourable expectations—the worker who first set the climate of work is remembered as the favourite.

In order to indicate the presence and extent of feelings of crisis and isolation at the time of referral, it will be shown that few families saw their relatives and friends as positively supportive, and attention will be drawn to the clarity with which the clients remembered their referral problems—a clarity which, if anything, has become more sharply focused with the years. These observations will be similar to a finding of George and Wilding (1972) in their study of motherless families.

It will be suggested further that the clarity and focus of clients' memories of referral are in contrast with the increasingly generalized recollections expressed by their social workers. This divergence has implications if one seeks to compare the views of clients and workers about the outcome of social work help, or if worker and client set out together to review the progress made in the case; for the base-line of referral means something different to both; and their perceptions of the base-line tend to diverge over time in quality if not in content.

Referral agents

The twenty-seven families were referred to the Family Service Unit by the routes shown in Table 2. The referral agent's importance lies not only in putting the client in touch with a source of help (or, perhaps, a source of further hardship) but also in the influence which, it is reasonable to suppose, he exerts upon the client's expectations about how he will be received, how he should respond, the kind of help or unhelpfulness he may expect, and the attitudes and procedures of individual workers and of the agency as a whole.

TABLE 2   Routes of referral for the twenty-seven families

from other social services	Children's Department	8
	Mental Health Department	4
	Probation Service	2
		14
from health services	Maternity and Child Welfare Clinic	1
	General practitioners	2
	Hospital	1
	School doctor	1
		5
from a vicar		1
from the Magistrates' Clerk's office		1
by the advice of a local newspaper		1
by self-referral and the advice of relatives or friends		5
		27

We had no direct way of discovering how families were prepared, if at all, for referral; the records of other services were not available, and might not in any case have assisted the study much in this respect. The families' recollections of their knowledge and expectations of the Unit's workers at the time of referral were available, however, and even allowing for considerable distortion of memory these recollections may provide some indication of the quality of referral procedures and may be shown to affect clients' evaluation of the Unit's work.

The families were asked two questions: what they expected the Unit to do and to be like in advance of receiving their first visitor; and whether or not they knew at that time that the Unit was a non-statutory service ('part of or different from the Town Hall services'). If we assume that respondents are likely to attribute to themselves more rather than less knowledge in their recollections, then their replies suggest a considerable lack of information about the Unit's work and inadequate care among referral agents. Of the fourteen clients referred by other social work services, seven knew that the Unit was a voluntary organization but, of these, four did not know what kind of help to expect. Of the seven who thought

REFERRAL, INTAKE AND HELP

the Unit was part of the statutory services, three did not know what help might be offered. On the other hand, of the five families referred by relatives and friends, four knew what help they might expect, but only two knew of the Unit's voluntary status.

In summary, the findings are as follows: seventeen families did not realize at referral that the Unit was separate from the 'Town Hall' services and, of these, seven had no idea what help might be offered to them or what attitudes they would encounter in the Unit's workers. Of the ten families who knew the agency's status, five did not know what to expect there. In all, the agency's functions, helping capacity and quality of work seem to have been wholly unknown to twelve of the twenty-seven families when they were referred there. The numbers involved in this study are small, but it seems possible that a client is more likely to have knowledge of an agency if referred by a friend or relative than if referred by another agency.

Fifteen families had some idea of what kind of help to expect at the time of their referral. These expectations may have been influenced in one or both of two ways: by knowledge directly gained from the referral agent; or by a projection of the clients' hopes concerning the alleviation of their problems. So far, emphasis has been placed on the importance of referral agents. In addition, relationship was established between the clients' recollected expectations and the crises, problems or needs which prompted the referral to the agency. Thus, among these fifteen families to the agency six stated that they expected material aid (Harris, Ilson, James, Roberts, Sheldon and Vincent), and also recollected their major needs in terms of financial or material hardship. Four families (Bailey, Cooper, Dell and Gordon) recollected that their primary need was for help in negotiating their debts; they defined their expectations of the Unit in these terms. Similarly, five families said that they expected to be helped by discussion of their difficulties (Lowe, Osborne, Price, Sanders and Underwood), and this expectation was consistent with the kinds of problems they presented —for example, depression, marital disharmony. In view of these findings, therefore, it is impossible to be sure whether the families' apparently realistic initial expectations of the Unit indicates good work by the referral agents or a subsequent tidying up of memories. In the latter case, the goodwill expressed by these clients towards the Unit might serve to encourage such realignments in their recollections.

Twelve families said that they had no idea what help or attitudes to expect at referral. Seven of these recall no hopes or feelings of any kind (Abbott, Charles, Milward, Norris, Tyson, Williams and Yates), but five recall approaching the Unit with negative feelings—

Mrs Francis knew it provided play groups for children, but this was not directly relevant to her problem; the Dimmock, Ewart, Kennedy and Stocks families variously recalled that at referral they felt afraid or suspicious, or both. Although it is reasonable to question the ways in which referrals were made in these cases, the preceding discussion suggests that the experience of referral may be a complex one. Examples may be taken from among these families of the possible complexities: Mrs Charles and Mrs Francis both liked the local authority social workers who referred them, but Mrs Charles's approach was complicated by a recent unhappy experience at another voluntary agency, while Mrs Francis was on particularly bad terms with the Supplementary Benefits Commission's officer; both at the time were separated (by choice or by prison) from their husbands, and enjoyed no support from family or friends; in the case of Mrs Francis, relationships with neighbours were also hostile. Similarly, the Kennedy family had no informal supports, their relationship with the SBC was a resentful one, and their immediate referral to the Unit by a Probation Officer from whom they sought help was, perhaps cynically, interpreted by them as lack of interest. Mrs Williams, coping alone while her husband was in prison, had had no previous contact with social workers; generally she got on well with the Officer of the SBC, but was referred to the Unit when he refused her application for a special needs grant. From these illustrations it would be reasonable to infer that factors other than what they were told (or not told) by referral agents contributed to an apparent ignorance of the Unit's work or to negative attitudes towards it. It seems likely that the experience of other relationships affects expectations and that scepticism or despair about the nature and solution of problems may have a negative effect on initial attitudes, just as hope appears to have had a positive one. It is appropriate to bear in mind these complexities as we consider two further factors: the extent and consistency of other sources of help; and the quality of the families' own efforts to solve their problems before and during the referral period. Neither seems to be a critically important factor in itself, but may be complementary to the influence of others.

The extent and consistency of other sources of help

On listening to the tape-recorded interviews, we were impressed by the comments of five families whose expectations of the attitudes of the Unit's workers (rather than merely of the forms of help available) seem to have been particularly realistic. It may be significant that the quality of their pre-referral relationships markedly differs from that indicated in the illustrations to the previous section, particularly in regard to the availability of informal and friendly support. Mr and Mrs James, for example, were on good terms with the local authority social worker who referred them, and already knew of the Unit's work through Mrs James's sister. Mrs Lowe was referred by a friend already in touch with the Unit; she said she had no contacts with social workers at that time, but was on poor terms with the SBC. Mrs Osborne, deserted by her husband, attempted suicide and was referred by her general practitioner whom she described as her 'only friend'; she had had no previous contact with social workers, but was on good terms with the SBC. Mr and Mrs Sheldon were referred by a friend who already knew of the Unit's work; they were at the same time on good terms with the local authority social worker, though not with the SBC. Finally, Mrs Underwood, in marital conflict, was self-referred, but knew about the Unit through her mother, who had received help several years before; she said she had no contact with social services.

Mayer and Timms (1970) have suggested that the availability of informal networks of support is a factor influencing a client's actively seeking help. Most clients of the FSU are not self-referred; and initially they are visited at home rather than expected to visit the Unit. These brief illustrations suggest, however, that informal supports (good relationships within the family of origin, close friendships, or 'good neighbours') may influence the client's expectation and perception of the Unit's attitudes in the early stages of work. It also seems possible that strong informal supports may help to offset hardship, not merely by compensating for inadequate help from the social services, but by providing some emotional stability in situations of inconsistency (or perceived inconsistency) in the attitudes of various services and 'helpers'.

The extent to which help is actually available from social services is difficult to assess. As has been suggested, the expectations of help which some clients brought to the Unit may have been distorted by negative relationships with other services. Such negative contacts cannot realistically be regarded as 'available help'. It seems necessary, therefore, to record not only the existence of contacts with other services but whether these services were judged by the clients as helpful, and, therefore, as 'available' emotionally as well as geographically and legally. In Table 3 each contact with a person, agency or institution which is remembered by the clients as available and helpful (or, at least, not unhelpful) is recorded with a plus sign (+); each contact remembered as available but disliked is recorded with a minus sign (−). In addition, positive and negative contacts are recorded in brackets when their availability has been ascertained from the case-records but was not recalled by the

TABLE 3 *The availability of other 'helpers'*

Family	Medical services	Church	Social services	Supplementary benefit	Education	Informal
Abbott	+		+(+)	+		
Bailey			+++−		(−) (+)	−
Cooper	+		+−	+		+
Charles	(+)		+−	−		
Dell	+		+−	−		−
Dimmock	(+) (+) (+)		+−(−)	+	(−)	
Ewart			(+)−(−)−(+)	−	(−)	+
Francis			++(+)(+)	−		
Gordon			++	++	(+)	−
Harris		+	++(+)−	−		
Ilson	+		+(−)		+	
James			+(+)	−		−
Kennedy			+*(−)(−)	−*		+−
Lowe			++	−		
Milward	+(+)	+	(+)	−		−†
Norris	(+)(+)	(+)	−	−	(−) (−)	−†
Osborne	+	+	+	+		++
Price			++			+
Roberts			+(−)	−*	(+) (−)	
Sanders			+(−)(−)	−*		
Sheldon			+	++		
Stocks	−*		−*			
Tyson	+		(−)			
Underwood			(+)	−*		−
Vincent			−*	+		++
Williams				+*		−
Yates	+		(+)(+)			

† This client made friends readily but lost them quickly and with accumulating feelings of loneliness.

families in interview. Note is taken also, by the same signs, of the quality of relationships with Social Security at the time of referral, and of the availability of informal supports. It should be noted in this last matter that a plus sign indicates the presence of family, neighbours or friends as helpful *in the experience of the family*; no attempt is made to judge the usefulness or acceptability of these contacts by other criteria. A minus sign indicates either physical isolation or that these contacts were experienced as unhappy, unkind or to be avoided. A blank space indicates that informal contacts were not mentioned by the respondents as relevant to their need for help. A single asterisk indicates that the Unit social worker's assessment of this relationship disagrees with the family's report of it.

It will be noted that, in effect, seven families were without help from social work services at the time of referral, and that—in their recollections—a further three did not consider that social work help was available to them. This does not imply that the services were out of touch or unwilling to help, but simply that they were not perceived as helpful in the situation of need. In addition, a majority of relationships with Supplementary Benefits Officers were described as negative ones. Where families were in touch with two or more social services (all referrals pre-dated the implementation of the Social Services Act), it rarely happened that their relationships were of similar quality. Most families, therefore, seem to have experienced some difficulties in relating to 'the authorities' or to have experienced these relationships as inconsistent. The families' social difficulties may well have been exacerbated by uneven, even contradictory, qualities in the simultaneous relationships of different authorities to the families concerned. We cannot judge whether these qualities were real in the perceptions of the social workers; but they were real to the families concerned, and the effects of these perceived incompatibilities upon the role-performances of workers and clients needs to be considered.

If one considers all the helping relationships available to the families, consistent support from both formal and informal sources, and without the intrusion of negative feelings, was available to only three families, one of whom was not in touch with any social workers at that time. Omitting consideration of informal influences, consistency is found in six cases.

Little is known about the effects upon those needing help of inconsistency and contradiction in the attitudes of those whose job it is to make help available. Assuming that more harm is achieved than good, the evidence provided by these families draws attention to an important but neglected aspect of social work practice. It will be suggested later in this chapter that the bewilderment and ambivalences of clients may have the effect of intensifying discrepancies in the attitudes of different 'helpers', and that the self-esteem of some social workers and other community helpers may become based upon increasingly discrepant attitudes, at the risk of further bewilderment and suffering for their clients.

The families' own efforts in coping

In addition to the help available from other sources and to the clients' hopes of further help arising from their referral to the Unit, an attempt was made to ascertain the ways in which families had tried to deal with their own problems. In all but two cases, the comments of the respondents, the social workers, the records, and —where available—letters from referral agents showed a high level of agreement. It is perhaps indicative of the emotional intensity of needs and the perceived seriousness of their plight that so many families could recall their feelings and efforts two, three, four or more years before the interviews; in no case did we encounter a devil-may-care attitude to the past.

Twelve families in all had made reasonable and thoughtful efforts to resolve their difficulties: the difficulties themselves may have been the outcome of recklessness, idleness or inadequacy, but the attempts to meet them were well-conceived even if unsuccessful. Seven families in particular (Harris, Lowe, Stocks, Underwood, Vincent, Williams and Yates) had made serious attempts to budget, had exerted themselves in various ways to make ends meet and to cope with their responsibilities without seeking additional help. Five families recognized their need for help, and sought it appropriately (Cooper, Ilson, Kennedy, Roberts and Sheldon).

A further five families had attempted to meet their problems—in their own admission and in the records—by unsatisfactory means: borrowing from money-lenders (Norris); making attempts at suicide as a protest against the inadequacy of their relatives or friends (Osborne, Price, Sanders); or by ignoring the problems (Abbott).

Eight families were wholly adrift, feeling incapable of exercising any influence upon the hopelessness of events (Bailey, Charles, Dimmock, Francis, Gordon, James, Milward and Tyson). Significantly, as will be discussed in the context of the clients' criteria of good and successful work, the capacity of the social worker to take control (of people as well as of events), to be firm, and to limit personal destructiveness, was widely referred to as a valuable attribute.

In only two cases (Dell and Ewart) were the accounts of the families and workers at variance with each other concerning the reasonableness of the clients' attempts to cope with their problems before referral.

Referral needs and the relevance of immediate help

So far we have considered influences and events in the lives of families before the intervention of the Unit's social workers. The assumption has been that the clients' perceptions of this intervention are influenced a great deal by preceding experiences and attitudes, which may be confirmed, offset, or possibly unaffected by what the social worker subsequently does. Whether the client regards the social worker as a saint or a nincompoop does not lie wholly within the sphere of influence of the worker. This may lead to a situation similar to the one discovered in this study, where the Unit's workers were highly praised by their clients and rarely, and only mildly, blamed; or to the alarming experience of an Education Welfare Officer who, by Mrs Norris's description in this study, had shown kindness to her family for many years, but who was regarded by the family with dislike or contempt. We may assume, however, that clients' evaluations of their social workers are at least partly influenced by what the workers do in relation to the clients' perceptions of their needs. In order to provide a focus for discussion with the families, an attempt was made in interview to establish with each the principal reason for referral to the FSU, the circumstances giving rise to the approach at that particular time, and the immediate response of the social workers: i.e. how they set out to help the family in the first week of contact, and the extent to which their efforts were judged to be relevant by the family.

Specifying the principal reason for referral presented for a few families difficult tasks of recall and precision. For example, it is appropriate to consider the case of Mrs Ilson, whose referral situation was the most complex: she came primarily for clothing, and expected to receive this kind of help; but the circumstances involved a history of bad relationships with her family of origin, separation from her husband, cohabitation (with her three children) with a Pakistani and pregnancy by him. She felt unable to obtain financial support from her husband for the children's maintenance in case he was able to discover where she lived. One child was suffering from asthma, another was beyond her control and was about to start school. She sought help for him from the Child Guidance Service, but, in her view, without success. She tried to keep a job but her wages were wholly absorbed by payments for the daily minding of the children. For Mrs Ilson, inability to afford children's clothing was the last straw. Clothes were refused by a

REFERRAL, INTAKE AND HELP

social agency to whom she applied, and she saw no alternative but to abandon her children. To record Mrs Ilson's presenting problem as one of material need must appear inadequate. One would expect any social worker in touch with her to have wider concerns than this and their failure to do so, as well as their refusal of clothing, may account for her continuing hostility towards the first social agency she approached. Similarly, we were frequently reminded by the social worker respondents in the national survey of FSU clientele

TABLE 4 *Referral needs*

	Open cases	Closed cases
Immediate material needs associated with unemployment (but no significant debts or emotional problems)	Ewart Harris James Kennedy	Roberts Vincent
Material needs and debts	Dell	
Material needs accompanying widowhood		Tyson
Material needs accompanying husband's imprisonment	Francis Gordon	Williams
Material needs accompanying desertion/separation	Ilson Lowe	Stocks
Debts (but no other immediate material or emotional problems)	Abbott Bailey Cooper	Sheldon
Debts associated with marital problems	Dimmock	Price
Debts associated with severe depression of wife	Milward Norris	Sanders
Suicidal thoughts/actions by wife, accompanying		
marital problems		Underwood
desertion	Charles Osborne	
widowhood		Yates

that specifying a single principal reason for referral distorted the complexity of their clients' needs, their own professional assessments, and their approach to helping. While sympathizing with this viewpoint, one must start somewhere, whether one is a social worker trying to help, or a client trying to make sense enough of his plight to present it coherently to the social worker. At any one time in the process of giving and receiving help, one seeks to find a focus for change or intervention, to establish a hierarchy of need or task. With the realization that it represents a simplification of the referral situation, Table 4 sets out the main needs recollected by the families.

Immediate material needs or debts were given primacy in twenty-three cases, and severe depression in the wife (usually amounting to thoughts of or attempts at suicide) was stated as the primary problem in four. A further three cases of severe depression in the wife are included among the families with debt problems.

The families were asked also to recount the kinds of help they remembered receiving in the first week of contact with the Unit. This help fell within three categories:

material aid (e.g. clothing, furniture, cash);
negotiating (e.g. with creditors, with the Supplementary Benefits Commission's officers, with employers, or with other agencies from which resources might be available);
emotional support (e.g. devoting a considerable amount of time and effort to clarifying the clients' expressions of feelings, and sharing these feelings).

Relating help to need

In twenty-five cases, the families reported complete satisfaction with the help received in response to their problems. In the remaining two cases, partial satisfaction was reported. No family reported serious discrepancy between the problem presented, help requested and help received. As this was an unexpected outcome—we considered the possibility of distortion in the replies received to the questions in this part of the study—it is appropriate to mention that subsequent interviews with the social workers supported this finding (twenty-five satisfied, one partly satisfied, one dissatisfied because 'she did not receive as much material aid as she asked for'). The findings were further supported by the records. Further study showed that it has been the practice of the workers in this Unit to meet their clients' needs in the mode in which they are presented, at once if possible (or with the least possible delay), irrespective of other kinds of help also being offered then or later.

The help offered may thus extend beyond what the client asks for or expects, but always includes some help of the kind requested. Thus, initial requests for material assistance are met, wholly or in part, without any extensive preliminary administrative checks which may delay the giving.

Two aspects of this approach will be considered from time to time in this study:

(1) its influence on the attitudes of families towards the Unit as a helping agency, and on their judgment of the social workers;
(2) use of material aid (as the reason for seeking help and as the worker's primary focus of helping) both as a symbol of more extensive needs, and as a predictive indicator of the worker's and agency's attitudes, and of the quality of future relationships in response to these wider needs.

Table 5 records the extent of correspondence between referral needs and the categories of help employed in the first week of work, as recollected by the families. It appears that a high degree of congruence existed in the recollections of the 'Open' group: i.e. eleven out of seventeen, compared with only three out of ten in the 'Closed' group. As none of the 'Closed' group expressed dissatisfaction, this may indicate a loss of memory of early events in a relationship which is now ended; in this respect it should be noted that in the cases marked with an asterisk (*) the records of the initial week's work indicated that the help was in fact congruent with the problems then presented.

In the comparison of evidence from families, social workers and records there was no major incompatibility. In the statements of eighteen families concerning the problems at referral, there was complete agreement with the records; and in the other nine cases, the only difference between respondents and records was that respondents fastened upon one particular and precisely detailed aspect of the problem-situation rather than (as in the records) reviewing the total range. Thus, for example, the Ewart, Gordon and Kennedy families had referred to their urgent material needs and to some debts, but not to other debts (including a threat of eviction). In a further five cases, the families had referred to material needs and debts but had not mentioned the marital disharmony present at the time (Abbott, Dell, James, Stocks, Williams). And in the final case (Yates), the family had omitted a reference to the near-delinquent behaviour of the children which had accompanied the depressive illness of the mother as a reason for referral.

It has been shown that in five cases, a remembered referral for material or financial difficulties subsumes marital difficulties.

TABLE 5 *Need and help*

'Material needs + unemployment' met by 'material aid + negotiating support'

	Open	Closed	
Congruent	Ewart		(N.B. a 'particularly satisfied' client)
Material aid only	Kennedy Harris James*	Vincent	

'Material needs + debts' met by 'material aid + negotiating'

	Open	Closed	
Negotiating only	Dell		(N.B. a 'satisfied' client, according to her response but regarded by the social worker as initially dissatisfied)

'Material needs + emotional difficulties' met by 'material aid + support'

	Open	Closed	
Congruent	Francis Gordon Ilson		
Material aid and negotiating	Lowe	Tyson* Williams*	
Emotional support		Stocks*	

'Debts' met by 'negotiating'

	Open	Closed	
Congruent	Abbott Bailey Cooper	Sheldon	(plus material aid) (immediate loan)

'Debts + marital/emotional problems' met by 'negotiating and support'

	Open	Closed	
Congruent	Norris		
Negotiating	Dimmock Milward*		(plus material aid)
Support		Price	(N.B. an 'unsure client' in terms of initial satisfaction; also received material aid)
		Sanders	

'Suicidal thoughts/actions' met by 'support'

	Open	Closed	
Congruent	Charles Osborne	Underwood Yates	(plus material aid)

Among these families, two (Stocks and Williams) seemed to acknowledge this indirectly when, in reply to a question concerning which aspect of the Unit's work they had found most helpful, they spoke in terms of emotional support rather than material aid. The other three, however, continued to speak of material help as the most valued help, and it is for this kind of help that they would, if appropriate, refer other families. Yet in all five cases, helping has included discussions of family relationship difficulties; and, indeed, all three families included a reference to emotional needs as lying within the most frequent areas of discussion during their contact with the Unit.

The simplest explanation of this apparent discrepancy is probably the family's wish to avoid reawakening a distressing (and possibly less acceptable) subject, especially in the presence of a stranger. Or it is possible in some cases that the marital tensions were exacerbated by material difficulties, and, in a sense, secondary to them. A further explanation is that, for some clients, material needs which are valid in themselves offer an opportunity for presenting, in a symbolic form, other unacknowledged needs. If this is so, then the way in which the social worker receives and deals with the material-needs presentation will provide the client with a symbolic indicator of regard for his less tangible needs. (Reference has been made to the policy of the Unit's workers in regard to their immediate response to the presentation of material needs.) Significantly, the help the clients had received with clothing, especially for the children (applicable in all but three cases), was the one form of help which no family forgot to mention, though relatively few placed this in an important position in relation to the other kinds of help available to them. The easy and ready way in which families first spoke of their application for material help could, superficially, be regarded as indicating merely a desire for hand-outs; but the evidence available—concerning the intensity of feelings in the referral-problem period, the help most appreciated by clients, and their definition of the relationships necessary to good social work —all indicates that material help *per se* was not the single primary objective for most of them, though it may have been presented in this way and may well have had a symbolic primacy.

It has been suggested that any distortion in clients' memories of their referral situation tends towards an intensification of the memory of one particular part of it. In contrast to this, the memories of social workers tend over time towards generalizing about, rather than precisely specifying, the clients' original needs. Thus, in speaking of the six families where their memories had suffered most distortion, the social workers tended to refer to general financial difficulties, rather than to the cutting-off of electricity, or to an eviction notice; they referred to the parents' anxiety about their children rather than to the children's precise and various needs.

These opposing tendencies would merit further study. It is suggested tentatively that, when workers and clients review together the effectiveness of the help given and received, they may all too easily, and without shared recognition, be relating their assessments of this help to diverging perceptions of their common baseline, the referral situation.

Some final comments concerning the influences exerted on clients' perceptions of the helpfulness of services

This chapter has been concerned to show how the relationships between many of the families and the social services (and other helpers) at the time of referral were uncertain and ambiguous: satisfactory with some and not with others. It has been suggested that these uncertainties, irrespective of the care or carelessness with which referrals were made to the Unit, may well have affected the attitudes and expectations of the families towards the Unit's workers, and even possibly the extent to which they recollected having any reliable knowledge in advance of the Unit's work. The experience of many families at the time of referral included uncertainty of relationships with 'the authorities', uncertainty about the response of future social workers, and anxiety about critical needs and about their personal inability to meet them. Comment has been made too about the unexpectedly high rate of satisfaction expressed by the families over the help received from the Unit in the first week of work; and this has been related to the congruence of initial help with the clients' verbal expressions of need.

My purpose at the close of this chapter is to take further two earlier comments: concerning the joint influence of all these factors upon the role-performances of both clients and social workers; and concerning the apparent neglect among social workers hitherto of the impact on their clients of concurrently incompatible or inconsistent attitudes expressed by 'helpers'; I suggested that possibly the self-esteem of some 'helpers' is based on the maintenance rather than resolution of incompatibility between services.

Pinker (1971) has pointed out our lack of information about the ways in which people define their relationships to the Social Services: 'we know almost nothing about the reasons for which citizens use services as they do, or about what attitudes lead them to feel deterred or encouraged in the search for assistance'. The present study suggests that this lack of knowledge is part of a wider problem: that there is no clear expectation that any citizens may reasonably hold concerning their reception by social services as a whole. Services do not appear to agree upon how their clients are expected to behave (or, at least, the clients themselves neither expect nor perceive any such tacit agreement), and even within a single agency two workers may, by their behaviour to clients, imply markedly different expectations. Ambivalence in seeking help is probably intensified, therefore, by clients' uncertainties about what constitutes appropriate client-behaviour in the eyes of different workers and different services. The fact that the business of seeking help takes place, for many clients, in situations of crisis (when sensitivity is heightened) increases both the ambivalences and the uncertainty, and may generate fear or hostility. It may be possible, by having regard to this situation as a whole, to explain some instances at least of what may otherwise appear as irrationality in the client: for example, the unexplained negative feelings which some families brought to their first contact with the Unit; the attitudes of Mrs Norris's family to the Education Welfare Officer; the unexpectedly small number of adverse comments we received about any aspect of the Unit's work.

Examples of initial feelings of ambivalence and fear were offered by the following respondents: Mrs Tyson said in an interview that she still feels a bit uncertain of her welcome at the Unit, in spite of the help she has received and her appreciation of it; Mr and Mrs Ewart, 'We were a bit threatened at first. We didn't know if they were going to take the kids off us, or what'; Mr and Mrs Sanders, 'In the early days, she (Mrs Sanders) used to say, "What's he coming round here for?"'; Mrs Gordon, 'I've had to put my pride in my pocket, you know.... I was very humiliated at first to have to ask for anything, but John (the FSU worker) put me more at ease.... Now I can ask for anything!'; Mrs Ilson, 'And then I started thinking: Where am I going? What will they think of me? They'll think I'm a beggar. But I *had* to go, I *wanted* to go. And then, when I went, they gave me some beautiful clothes for the children. *Then* I was thinking: how can I repay?—taking with one hand, and not giving back with the other.'

Mrs Ilson's comment well illustrates a state of uncertainty about the nature of the client-role, and the resulting intensification of ambivalence towards receiving help. It is suggested that ambivalence and uncertainty of this order of intensity may be resolved by the splitting of responses, so that some workers (or agencies) receive positive projections from the client while others receive negative ones. In this case, whether a social worker receives positive or negative projections will depend on his activities and attitudes in the early stages of the case, more than on the quality of his work over a period of time.

It will be shown in a later chapter that feelings about the intake worker, for good or ill, overshadow the clients' impressions of all but the most recent other workers, and attention will then be paid to the qualities of relationship which assist a social worker's acceptance as an immediately helpful person. But in addition to the worker's personality and skills, any of the agency's administrative procedures or constraints which affect the speed and scope of a worker's initial response to expressed need may help to determine whether that worker and agency receive positive or negative projections. The informality of the Unit's administrative structures, its wide range of services speedily available, and the small caseloads permitting frequent and long home visits, could help to explain why the families interviewed held the Unit's workers in high esteem, irrespective, perhaps, of the intrinsic qualities of their helping. That their clients' esteem may have been partly the outcome of a defensive emotional manoeuvre against critical uncertainty would assist the explanation of the single greatest discrepancy between the replies of the social workers and the families. This concerned the extent to which the clients felt they could speak their minds honestly to the workers.

In the interviews, and in listening to the recordings, we could detect no insincerity in the replies of twenty-five families that they could always speak honestly; the social workers, by contrast, felt that only in a few families was such honesty actually presented to them in their day-to-day work. It is as if, driven by an early crisis of feelings into close and dependent relationships with the social workers, the families felt under an inner compulsion still to project total acceptability upon the workers when reviewing their association from its critical beginnings: even though (and this is to the credit of the workers concerned) the daily experience of relationships is latterly much less close and dependent than it was at first.

Some critics of social work assume that social workers set out to establish an increasingly intense relationship with their clients. The evidence of the present study suggests that social workers are sometimes confronted *ab initio* with a demand for intense relationship, and exercise their skills to reduce this intensity rather than to maintain or enhance it. This is an area of day-to-day practice where the assumption that casework and psychoanalytic techniques are closely associated could be shown to be glib, plausible and wrong.

A more serious danger lies, however, in the possibility that the effects of ambivalence and splitting—the endowment of social workers with projected positive or negative feelings—may be intensified and given irreversible permanence. Social workers held in affection may collude with, and increase, the clients' negative feelings (and sometimes fantasies) about mistrusted workers. Those held in mistrust may equally over-react to and thus intensify their clients' professions of dislike. Examples of this are the elements of jolly or vindictive gamesmanship expressed by some social workers about Social Security officers or, indeed, towards the members of any other service. One may detect similar attitudes sometimes between community workers and caseworkers. A social worker may find that, in expediting the services of another agency (or even just in talking about it), the gratitude and praise he receives are disproportionate to his actions, and are matched by the expression of disproportionate hostility towards the other service. This hostility can hardly ever be resolved by the mistrusted agency, however positive that agency's intentions may be. Any good thing the client subsequently receives will be cynically regarded as the effect of the competent intervention or helping of the beloved worker. Hostility may be increased in this transaction as much by the giving as by the withholding of help; either way, the loved worker becomes more loved. Only with difficulty can he resolve the client's hostility to the other agency, and his self-esteem may prevent his wishing to do so.

Yet if some resolution is not found, clients whose needs are chronic or repetitive are thrust more deeply, with each renewal of need, into a hostile position against what may be an essential source of help. On each occasion, they will feel the need for further mediation by the worker held in affection. So dependency is intensified and the ambivalence about needing help, similarly intensified, is again split and projected so as to ensure greater affection for some workers and greater hostility for others.

From the present study, the activities of two (well-liked) Unit workers when confronted with such situations, may be inferred from the comments of Mr and Mrs Sheldon and Mr Vincent. Mr and Mrs Sheldon had moved from a position of extreme hostility to Social Security about four years ago to one of co-operation, and the FSU played an important part in this movement: 'I think it's a lot better now than it was. If I have to go to Social Security now, they've got my case history there, and they deal with me straightaway.' Mr Vincent was in touch with the Unit for a much shorter time because of periods of imprisonment, but from the first he readily accepted his worker's guidance and criticisms, however adverse the latter might be. Of other services he said this: 'When I was in prison, the Welfare Officer said, "Do you want us to have a talk to your wife?" "No," I said, "I don't want you to get help to the wife; we've got a home, and we've got the Unit." And when I said that, their attitude changed completely. They *detest* the Unit. They're jealous to death of them. Probation

Officers, Welfare Services—you name them, they're jealous to death of them. As soon as you say you're in touch with the Unit, they're jealous to death of them.'

There is need for further study of the ways in which ambivalence and uncertainty in seeking help can lead, through the influences of referral agents, intake workers and administrative practices, to situations where a client's spontaneous responses reflect projections of affection or mistrust of such intensity as to seem irrational. There is the further need to investigate the collusions and re-inforcements that these projections may encourage in 'helpers' of all kinds, and the ways whereby the worker's response to the client's projections may, with the best will in the world, be antagonistic to the welfare and independence of the client.

Notes

George and Wilding's (1972) study of fathers managing alone demonstrated that those needing services lacked the usual range of family supports, or were unable to accept these supports (pp. 140, 151). The present study, with a different client-group, supports this finding. George and Wilding noted also the clarity of their respondents' memories of their initial problems, as we have found among the FSU families. The memories of the social workers for referral problems, on the other hand, seem to become less precise than those of their clients.

Kadushin (1972) has related the successful outcome of casework to congruence between the worker's mode of helping and the client's way of stating his problems. The present study indicates a high level of congruence, both in the first week of help and in continuing work. For the reasons indicated in Chapter 7, however, this congruence has been related to the clients' feelings of satisfaction rather than to the concept of success.

Reference should be made to Mayer and Timms (1970) for several findings closely paralleled to the present study: e.g. the congruence of expectations of clients and workers (pp. 9-10, 79); clients' expectations on approaching the agency (pp. 66 *et seq*.); the reluctance attached to being a client, and to seeking material help (p. 102, pp. 99-105); the frame of reference which previous helpers have provided for the expectations of clients (p. 152); and the influence of informal resources (Chapter 3).

A further study relevant to the present discussion is McKay *et al.* (1973). Among clients of a Social Services Department, just under a third do not know what to expect at the time of intake.

It has been implied in this chapter that, for several families, referral to the Family Service Unit took place at a time of crisis when the dominant emotion was panic. The presence of panic is suggested also by the clarity and emotional accompaniment of clients' memories, as recorded in Chapters 5 and 6 and in Appendix VI. The expressed need for firmness and control from the social worker, to which reference is made in Chapter 6, may be a further sign of these nearly uncontrollable feelings. Dockar-Drysdale (1973) has defined panic as 'unthinkable stress': it will be noted later that for many clients time to express themselves was an important benefit of interviews; given time and a willing listener, it became possible to make panic thinkable and containable. Appendix IV shows that several families discussed 'daily events'; sometimes these were of a trivial and repetitive kind. Many social workers would agree, however, that discussion of small events—sometimes of a minute-by-minute account of daily life—is described as helpful by clients who feel temporarily disorganized and panicky, or whose lives are experienced as unstructured or meaningless.

4
Continuing help

This chapter is concerned with the activities and discussions which went into helping the families and with the perceptions and memories of relationships between them and their social workers. Bearing in mind that social work is built up of interchanges and transactions, I propose to give equal weight to the views of clients and workers, without supposing a greater awareness in one or the other of what was happening between them. This approach is open to the objection that I have thus denied the professional expertise of the social workers. Certainly this objection would be valid if my purpose were to appraise the professional quality of help offered by the various workers; but I do not intend to imply in this study that the employment of any particular modes of work was, in professional terms, more or less appropriate. My concern is with what the participants perceived to be taking place rather than with evaluating or judging the quality of the processes of help.

It is important to clarify this matter for two reasons: first, so that the reader will discount any professional preferences which I may unwittingly imply; and second—and more important—because many of the aspects of work which will be discussed are such as one would expect, in another context, to find in an *evaluation* of casework practice. The reader may therefore be led to assume that an evaluative exercise is intended when it is not. For example, I shall describe, through the eyes of clients and workers, some of the techniques employed in helping; some aspects of the personalities of the social workers will be set down as described by their clients; the workers' perceptions of changes in social functioning during the period of their contact with the families will be recorded. If this were to be an evaluation of social work practice, however, such information would need supplementing in three ways: by objective description of the clients, by the establishment of criteria by which functional changes could be both measured and correlated to helping procedures, and by some analysis of various dimensions in the personalities of the social workers. This supplementary information is not available. Thus, the work, the social changes, and the personal qualities described in this study should be regarded as subjective to the people directly concerned in the processes of help. Later descriptions of 'good' and 'successful' work will be of the same quality. I hold the view, however, that subjective information of this kind is interesting in its own right, and should form part of any evaluation of the practice of social work.

The scope of help offered and the subjects discussed

All who have visited a barber, a dentist or a lawyer will recognize that the services offered and the subjects discussed are not co-terminous. Discussions may be experienced as helpful (as providing, say, the discharge of pent-up feelings, or the name of a good plumber), but may not be directly related to the service sought or formally offered. It is less clear whether the same distinction may be drawn in relation to visits to psychiatrists or to members of other professions which subsume a variety of ideologies of treatment; but, in most such cases, receptionists or nurses are available for supplementary discussions outside the specifics of professional help. In the present study, families were asked to recount the kinds of help they had received, and were later asked to recall the subjects which were most frequently discussed with the Unit's social workers. Similar questions were asked of the social workers, and finally the case-records were searched in order to verify, dispute or supplement the information received. A large measure of agreement was discovered between families, workers and records as to the scope and categories of help offered, though examples within these categories were sometimes overlooked or withheld. Less congruence was found in the recollections of clients and workers of the subjects most frequently discussed. It seems best, therefore, to separate 'help' and 'discussion' as far as possible in recording the findings.

The kinds of help offered and received were grouped, as recorded for the first week's work, into three categories:

(1) direct material aid of various kinds (including money);
(2) negotiations by the social worker on behalf of the family; to this was added the management of resources and debts, as family budgeting is frequently related to external negotiations of some kind;
(3) help through discussion: in this category a distinction was drawn between

TABLE 6 *The categories and scope of help*

Family	Material aid				Negotiation and management			Other provisions		Relationship quality		Advice		Aspects of befriending					
	Clothes	Furniture, bedding	Short-term loans	Toys, Xmas food	Negotiating	Debt-collecting/payment	Budgeting	Holidays, day-trips	Groups	'Professional'	Befriending	Contraception/FPA	Child-care	Accompanying to court	Doctor/hospital	Prison	Shopping	Standing bail	Teaching to read
Abbott	X	(X)	(X)	X	(X)			X			X	(X)							
Bailey	X	X	X		(X)			X											
Cooper	X			X	X	X	X			X	X								
Charles	X	(X)	(X)			X	X	X	X	(X)	X								
Dell	X	(X)	X	X		X	X			X	X								
Dimmock	X	(X)	(X)	X	X	(X)	X	(X)	X	X	(X)		(X)	X	X				
Ewart	X	X	X		X	X	(X)	(X)	(X)	(X)	X	(X)						X	
Francis	X	X			X	X	(X)		X	X	X								
Gordon	X	(X)	(X)		X	(X)	X		X	X	X			X					

	C1	C2	C3	C4	C5	C6	C7	C8	C9	C10	C11	C12	C13	C14	C15	C16	C17	C18
Harris						(X)		x		(X)	(X)	x		x			x	x
Ilson						(X)	(X)	x	x	x	x	x		x			(X)	x
James				(X)			(X)	x		x	x	x		x			(X)	x
Kennedy								(X)	x	(X)	(X)			x		x	x	x
Lowe		x						x		x	x	x	(X)	x		(X)	x	x
Milward					x			x	x	x	x	(X)	(X)	x		(X)	x	x
Norris								(X)	x	x	x	(X)	x	x		x	x	
Osborne				(X)		(X)	(X)	x	(X)	(X)			(X)	(X)				
Price	(X)			(X)					x	x	x	(X)		x			x	
Roberts														(X)	x			x
Sanders								(X)				(X)	x	x	x		x	x
Sheldon			x			(X)	(X)	x	x			x	(X)	(X)		x	(X)	x
Stocks			(X)				(X)	x				(X)	(X)	(X)		(X)	(X)	x
Tyson								x	x					x				x
Underwood						(X)		x		x		x		x	x		x	x
Vincent					x	(X)		x	(X)			x	x	x	x	x		x
Williams			x					x	(X)			x		x		(X)		x
Yates								x	x			x		x			(X)	

(i) discussions recognized by clients and workers as related to feelings in a specific and 'professional' way, and
(ii) discussions recognized by both as indication of friendliness (i.e. less specific to problem-solving and not experienced by the worker as requiring self-discipline, nor by the client as effecting specific emotional change), together with some reference to the practical help included in the notions of friendliness or befriending.

Fourth and fifth categories were added:

(4) the provision of group experiences of various kinds (play groups, mothers' groups, social or education groups for adolescents) and holidays or day-trips;
(5) the giving of direct advice: this somewhat unsatisfactory category was added during the records-search, when isolated pieces of advice-giving were discovered which could not, for lack of corroboration, be related to the subcategories of 'professional' discussion or befriending.

Table 6 broadly indicates the kinds of help made available to individual families. The families' recollections are indicated by x. So far as could be ascertained, no families produced false memories. Separate notation was not necessary for the recollections of the social workers, for these mainly fell within the scope of the families' responses, though frequently they were less precisely remembered. Supplementary information, mostly from the records, is indicated by (x).

It will be noted that material aid was made available in some measure to all families save one. In addition, all families received regular invitations to jumble sales and to Christmas sales of toys and games. The forms of material aid most commonly provided were clothing and furniture. Twenty-four families had received clothing, and none overlooked to mention this in interviews; in almost every case, clothing was the first form of help stated. (No check-list of the various forms of help was used in interview, and families were wholly dependent on their powers of recall.) By contrast, thirteen of the twenty-two families who had received furniture, and nine of the thirteen who had received grants or loans, did not mention them in their recounting of help. In explanation of the latter, it is possible that loans and grants were a sensitive area of admission, likely not to be mentioned in the absence of a check-list. An illustration of this sensitivity was provided by Mrs Ewart, describing her feelings when a social worker gave her a loan but told her not to return for more. 'I don't think he realized what he'd said. He didn't take our word. He was rotten, rotten. He should never have said what he did.' It is more difficult to understand why furniture was so frequently overlooked or forgotten by the families, and also by the social workers, compared with the giving of clothes. Tentative explanations which seem to fit the facts are, first, that clothing is made available from a well-supplied and well-ordered store at the Unit, more-or-less on demand; furniture takes longer to obtain because of storage difficulties and therefore is seldom available at the moment of need. Second, it was evident from direct observation during the research interviews that the quality of the clothing was far better than that of the furniture: several families spoke warmly of the excellence of the clothing, its surpassing their expectations and what they could have hoped to afford in the shops; furniture was mentioned with appreciation but not enthusiasm. Finally, the provision of clothing, by its immediate readiness at times of crisis (often at the first interview and periodically for several years), may well have assumed symbolic connotations of a caring relationship: Mrs Tyson described how extremely upset she felt when the caseworker once forgot to bring the clothes she had promised, and she sounded surprised at the strength of her own reaction.

Help with various kinds of negotiation was available to twenty-four families, and was mentioned by twenty. Proportionately fewer spoke of the Unit's workers' collecting and paying weekly instalments of debts, or of help with the budgeting of money (ten out of seventeen and fourteen out of twenty-one respectively), though both kinds of help were described appreciatively by all who mentioned them. As Mrs Abbott commented, 'You can't keep the family together if the money's not straight.' Mr Vincent remarked that if he paid his debts direct to his creditors rather than by a single payment in the social worker's weekly home visit, the bus fares involved would amount to a considerable weekly sum. It was evident from the replies of several respondents that the social worker's weekly debt-collection represented a hidden form of direct material aid. Mrs Price recognized that a moral dilemma is raised for the agency in this particular respect when she emphasized that, in her view, the Unit's resources should be related as directly as possible to the needs of children rather than of parents; parents expect too much of them—they expect them to pay the bills.

It has been noted that forms of help involving the transfer of money were less frequently mentioned by families than the considerably less time-consuming non-financial negotiation or mediation undertaken by the social worker on the families' behalf. Furthermore, financial transactions were referred to less by the 'closed' than by the 'open' families. It may be that, as in the earlier matter of loans and grants, any financial transactions are sensitive areas of admission. Possibly, too, the collecting of debts was a regular, almost automatic, procedure easily taken for granted. Moreover, it became evident from the replies of both families and social workers that negotiation is perceived as a more dramatic business than budgeting. Collecting a weekly debt seemed, for both sides, to be 'just part of the job', whereas obtaining work for a discharged prisoner, raising a special needs grant, disarming a creditor, or preventing an eviction were seen as substantial, even glamorous, tasks, and ones in which the notions of 'successful' and 'good' were most frequently employed by clients to describe both the work and the worker. Negotiation was seen by some clients as service 'beyond the call of duty', and as an indicator of the moral worth of the caseworker. Patient and reliable debt-collecting seemed to carry no such moral value, unless combined during home-visits with evidence of concern and caring related to non-financial matters. Social workers—as will be shown in a later chapter—were morally judged by their expressions of interest in the general well-being of family-members (their friendliness, in effect) rather than by their maintenance of essential but humdrum tasks.

Thirteen families contained children who had been on camping holidays provided by the Unit's staff. In addition, the parents were taken by car to spend a day with their children during the camp. All the parents interviewed spoke of the camps as the only chance of a holiday their children would have, and Mrs Price suggested longer-term benefit than this when she said of the camps and play groups, 'Children need them to get their minds stable for when they are older'.

Eighteen families had made use of the play groups, mothers' groups and teenagers' groups regularly held at the Unit. Most of the mothers in the twenty-seven families had received invitations for themselves and their children: some were too shy to attend, but others—notably Mrs Norris, Mrs Gordon and Mrs Williams—saw the mothers' groups as vitally important opportunities for sharing problems and learning from others. Mrs Norris explained that as the demand for the meetings is greater than the space available, so the mothers have to take it in turns to attend: she regretted that she could no longer go because it was not her turn. Mrs Gordon described the support given by the group meetings in helping individual members to manage their own lives: 'We go to a mothers' group ... we have a good time. It seems to *relax* you somehow. It makes you realize that other people have got troubles as well as you. And you talk—but we don't talk in particulars [i.e. we do not always talk about our personal affairs]. Actually, on Tuesday we were talking about death, of all things.

Perhaps because I lost my father-in-law on Saturday.... I'd got it on my mind.' (Interviewer: 'But it gives you a relaxed feeling to talk about it?') Mrs Gordon: 'Oh yes. Well, there's one of them, she was *very* inhibited when she came; she hardly said a thing. And when she did, she stuttered a bit—nerves. And we slowly brought her round, and we finally found out who the trouble is. And she straightened it out herself. It was her mother kept coming on to her—interfering all the time. It wasn't her house, it was more her mother's from what I gathered. But she kicked her out, more or less! ... She says they've put curtains up on the wall [round her child's bed], and she said "My mother would never have tolerated that." But she said it looks lovely, and the little lass is really pleased with it. I said, "They're *your* children." And she seems a lot more relaxed.' Mrs Williams also described how the group had helped to foster her self-confidence: 'Why I liked it best [was]—[if] you go to anywhere and your husband's in prison, they more-or-less look down on you. *I* think they do, anyway. But there [at the group], there was somebody.... [we were] all in the same position; you know—not bragging and brawling, just all —*poor off*, and all in the same boat. You could discuss things with one another; you know, things that you couldn't get off your chest round here. You could discuss them there and get them all off your chest.'

Only one family volunteered a dislike for meeting other clients at the Unit; the husband in particular, although he visited the Unit for strictly personal discussions with the social worker or when the family needed clothes, did not like associating with other families there. As feelings about visiting the Unit were not specifically explored with all the families, we cannot be sure how many others felt as this family did. In all, four families (one 'open', three 'closed') never visited the Unit. Of those needing clothes, nineteen families visited the Unit for them, while five relied on the worker bringing them. Of these five, three of the mothers brought their children to play groups, but preferred not to use their regular visits as an opportunity to visit the clothing store (which operated like a shop, so that several other people might be present).

Less than half the families (twelve) made visits to the Unit for interviews, or at times of crisis, or for informal discussion with their social workers. For these purposes, the telephone was more frequently used than a visit to the office, even among families who came regularly to group meetings or to the clothing-store. Unit House seems to have been regarded as a centre for practical facilities rather than as a place for individual discussions. Except among the families who particularly valued the emotional support of the group meetings (rather than their recreational aspects), the home-visit was seen by all clients, and indeed by all the workers, as the principal focus for the Unit's work.

The emphasis placed on home-visiting as the central focus of work, the importance of weekly collections of instalments against debts, and—in some families—the regularity of crises, all combine to maintain a high frequency of home-visits, and thus of interviews, throughout the period of a case. Contact between workers and clients does not change in either frequency or location as it does, for example, in the probation and aftercare service. Among the twenty-seven families, three had been, or still were, visited regularly more than once a week throughout the whole period of contact; twenty-two were visited weekly and occasionally more often; only two families were visited as seldom as once a fortnight.

When asked to recount all the major subjects of discussion, therefore, most clients momentarily despaired: discussions were so frequent over so long a period that they were experienced as covering virtually the totality of their lives. Three or four could not get beyond this feeling of totality, but among the rest, material needs, money and debts were most often mentioned first— inevitably, perhaps, in those families where workers collected a weekly sum of money. The health or feelings of the wife were the next most frequently mentioned topics; and, in third place, something to do with the care or health of the children. Few families (four) mentioned marital problems, but these were judged to be major areas of discussion by the social workers in eleven further families; and the records of work with an additional four families indicated that a fair amount of discussion had taken place at some time, though possibly not recently. Marital difficulties or tensions formed a significant part of the discussions with nineteen families, therefore, but were rarely listed by families among the primary subjects, and, as has been shown, were seldom presented as the primary problem at the time of referral. It is also of interest, as possibly indicative both of the focus of family casework practice in general (not only at the Sheffield Unit) and of the expectations of clients, that the feelings, health and problems of the husbands were mentioned as important by only two families and five workers.

A table of replies concerning the major topics of discussion in interviews is set out as Appendix IV. It will be seen that the recollections of the social workers enlarged but did not dispute the memories of the clients. The records enlarged both but did not in any case call into question what had been said in the research-interviews.

In social work practice, avoidance and dishonesty in discussions are important aspects of interviews. In the last chapter it was recorded that all clients said they were 'able to speak their minds' in interviews: certainly the impression was given that they could discuss any subject with their social workers. Although the social workers doubted the high degree of honesty described by the clients, they confirmed that, so far as they could tell, eighteen families did not avoid discussion of any important matters affecting the functioning of the family. Three of these eighteen families held back information in a few limited areas: two because of anxiety about the worker's disapproval, and one for fear of upsetting the worker. (The first two concerned the commission of offences, and the last related to the suppression of angry feelings about something the social worker had done.) The wife in a further family lied once about her address when she left her husband for a short period.

In six families, the workers considered that husband, wife or both had regularly and deliberately avoided all discussion of the central problem of marital disharmony, and in three of these had occasionally held back information in limited areas such as debt, school attendance and criminal offences. One of these six families had also avoided discussion of the wife's health because of her fear of cancer.

In only three families did the social workers consider that the parents had persistently avoided all discussion of their general responsibilities for their children and for each other.

Dishonesty was considered to have seriously complicated the help offered to seven families; and in a further six there had been occasions when information essential to effective help had been withheld. In general therefore, the workers appear to have enjoyed a high level of their clients' confidence and honesty in about half their work.

Table 7 sets out the subjects given primacy as the single most important topic of discussion in each family. It will be noted that there is close agreement between the replies of the families and the social workers in twelve cases. For the rest, money matters (i.e. material lack, debts), the health and feelings of the wife, and the care of the children are the most frequent areas of concern. The wife's feelings and health were given first place by eleven families and, in the view of the social workers, should be given first place in three others. (Her health is specifically mentioned as the primary topic in five out of twenty-seven families, either alone or in conjunction with problems in feelings.)

An important conclusion therefore, seems to be, that, although this area of concern accounted for only a few of the original referrals, and seemed relatively unimportant when clients and workers considered the scope of help needed and offered, nevertheless it occupied a considerable amount of interviewing time. This may, in part, arise from the greater frequency with which

TABLE 7 *The subjects most frequently discussed*

Family	Family's view	Worker's view, if different
Abbott	care of children	family life as a whole
Bailey	money matters	marital tensions
Cooper	money matters	
Charles	wife's feelings	care of children
Dell	immediate crises	
Dimmock	(don't know)	wife's health
Ewart	immediate crises	
Francis	wife's feelings	money matters
Gordon	family health	housing and money matters
Harris	old times, and money	
Ilson	(don't know)	marital interaction
James	wife's feelings	
Kennedy	wife's feelings	children's health
Lowe	money matters	
Milward	wife's feelings	
Norris	money matters	wife's health
Osborne	wife's feelings and health	
Price	wife's feelings	
Roberts	(don't know)	care of children
Sanders	wife's feelings	(agreed) *and* support to husband
Sheldon	money matters	
Stocks	money matters	wife's feelings and health
Tyson	wife's health	housing problems
Underwood	wife's feelings	
Vincent	problems with the authorities	husband's unemployment
Williams	care of children	marital tensions
Yates	wife's feelings and management	family relationships

wives (rather than husbands) are interviewed alone. But this is only a partial explanation: the national survey showed that, in the views of the social workers, ill-health forms an important problem area, not merely a frequent talking-point. One way of looking at this would be by distinguishing between wants and needs, or by reviving the currently unfashionable terms 'presented problems' and 'underlying problems'. Certainly, in the families' views, their *problems* were most frequently concerned with material needs and debts; these were discussed regularly, and the Unit was regarded as a helpful agency because of the immediacy of its concern with these problems. But in only seven families was this the *principal topic* in interviews; the greater need seems to have been to discuss the well-being of the wife. It will be noted later in this chapter that, when they were asked to recall the most helpful qualities of the help they had received, families mentioned emotional support and reliable friendship with greater frequency than the referral problems and referral circumstances would have led us to predict. This finding accords well, however, with the analysis of interview-content, rather than of problems brought and help requested.

Professional help and help through friendship

A distinction was drawn in the categories of help offered (and in the tabulation) between discussions of a professional kind and discussions of a friendly kind. This is at best a rough-and-ready distinction for a variety of reasons. The personality and skills of the social worker and the feelings of the client about his needs and experiences all help to influence whether the processes of help are deemed to be professional or friendly. Moreover, as the following chapter will show, the experience of a relationship largely determines how a service is perceived by both parties to it. Thirdly, in view of current developments among social workers of a variety of operational models (various not only in methods and techniques but also in the extent to which they affirm or deny professionalism), one is hard put to it to judge, with any hope of agreement from one's colleagues, what constitutes a professional attitude or task. Several social workers described the different degrees of friendliness they felt for different clients in such a way as to suggest that appropriate actions, comments or questions might be the outcome of spontaneous goodwill in one case and of professional judgment in another. Mayer and Timms (1970) draw a distinction, however, between 'functionally specific' relationships and 'diffuse' relationships, and something similar is attempted here in the differentiation of two kinds of helping-through-discussion. In the interviews and in reading the case-records, indications were sought of instances when a worker had employed self-discipline and skill in patient and careful listening, prompting and commenting with the conscious intention of encouraging the therapeutic expression of unhappy feelings; and situations were sought where emotional dependence had been consciously accepted with a view to bringing about modification in clients' outlook, attitudes and capacities to cope with inner or external stresses. Instances of these kinds were tentatively regarded as 'professional' help for the purpose of this analysis.

Befriending or friendliness, by comparison, refers here to essentially spontaneous acts, requiring no qualities of relationship other than one would expect to find among friends: for example, dependability, appropriate cheerfulness, sympathy. Implicit also is the possibility of reciprocity of help and interest.

Some families seemed to see their social workers more as friends who know about the social services—occasionally as friends with power—than as people doing a job (professional or not), and most used the words 'friend' or 'friendly' when talking of the social workers. Three families in particular, while recognizing that the workers were doing a job, considered that friendliness was a prerequisite for it. Thus, Mr and Mrs Sanders said of one worker whom they regarded as unsatisfactory: 'He didn't seem so warm. He gave you the impression that it was just his job, and he wasn't really interested. He gave you the impression that he'd majored in this subject at university without actually going into people's *feelings* ... he'd just *sit* there. He'd say, "The only thing to do is to cut corners," and I'd say to him, "Well, we'll starve if we cut corners any more. We can't do the impossible. Nobody can do the impossible."' Here, it might be argued, the problem may not have been lack of friendliness, but inadequate empathy in the relationship, inappropriate choice or use of interviewing skills, or misjudgment of needs and resources. But Mr and Mrs Sanders saw the difficulty as someone just doing a job, rather than being friendly, implying that friendliness was essential to effectiveness. This social worker also gave advice which, in their terms, was irrelevant and therefore unhelpful.

Mr and Mrs James received visits from a student at one period: he also gave advice, and was disliked for it because this was seen as a lack of warmth as well as lack of understanding. 'We didn't like him. He said he was on a course. He didn't seem to listen. We never seemed to *talk* about things. He used to keep changing the subject.' Mrs Gordon described another social worker as 'quite good—they've all been good' but 'it seemed as though she was standoffish ... to me, she wasn't *really* interested'.

Yet, in all three cases, the records prepared by these social workers indicated considerable concern about how to be helpful: the inappropriate advice, perceived lack of interest, and standoffishness were all amply denied by the warmth and concern expressed in the records. Neither was there evidence in the records to suggest that these workers were preoccupied with the development of a specifically professional rather than friendly relationship. A likely explanation—and, if true, an important one for social work education—was that lack of skill was in each case identified by the families as lack of concern. Here and elsewhere I could find no support for the view that, in the perceptions of the families as they received help, 'professional' help-through-discussion was aloof or cool while 'friendly' help-through-discussion was 'warm'. If the worker's help and expressions of concern were perceived as appropriate and relevant, then he was regarded as friendly; if not, then, irrespective of his own feelings and intentions, he was regarded as unconcerned and emotionally remote. It is possible, of course, that concern and unconcern may both be present at the same time: one in the awareness of the social worker, and the other unwittingly exemplified in what he says and does. But whatever the explanation, these three cases (and others) illustrate the difficulty of drawing a distinction between professional help and help through friendship, especially when the person perceived as a friend is professionally employed.

Within the limitations set by conceptual and perceptual problems, no discrepancy was detected between the recollections of the social workers and families of the kinds of help offered and received, either in material or emotional terms. The workers' comments, recorded as (x), are supplementary, not alternative, to the comments of the clients. This being so, it will be clear that the social workers regarded friendliness as the normal context for offering help. As we have seen from notes on the referral situations of these families several lacked the support of relatives, neighbours and friends, and it may be that the social workers spontaneously filled this kind of role. The three families where friendliness was not regarded (by clients or workers) as part of the help received were: Mr and Mrs Bailey, for whom financial and relationship crises were so frequent that all concerned in them recognized the need for the exercise of more continuous emotional control than would have been compatible with friendship; Mr and Mrs Dell, with whom the social worker deliberately maintained an emotional 'distance' because of the presence of a manipulative and, in the worker's view, self-destructive form of dependence; and Mrs Price, whose marital difficulties were long-standing, whose husband resented his wife's association with the Unit, and who needed special help to come to terms with a situation she could not hope to change.

In work with six families, befriending was the workers' means of helping: these were situations where a more intensive kind of help with feelings was considered to be irrelevant, in that no significant emotional adaptation seemed necessary (Abbott, Sheldon), or where it was considered that an exploration of the feelings of one or more members might adversely affect their precarious stability in relation to each other.

It will be noted also that befriending involved, in some cases, giving advice which, in the view of the social workers, was acceptable essentially because of its context of friendship. It has been suggested already that some families do not like people who give advice; and what the social workers described as advice was described by some clients as suggestion. It will be shown, however, that, whichever word is used to describe this form of help, it was often accompanied by considerable firmness and by the establishing of controls or limits on the part of the social workers; and that these were usually appreciated rather than resented by clients. It appears, therefore, that what was in effect the same mode of help may have been described as 'advice' when resented and 'suggestion' when approved, and that the client's perception of friendliness or friendship in the worker may have been influential in determining this designation. This will be discussed further in the next chapter. A reminder, however, of the complexity of these apparently simple concepts is provided by the inclusion, in the tabulation of help offered, of advice about contraception and the care of children as aspects of befriending. From discussion with the workers concerned, it was evident that this advice was given not in response to the questions of the clients, but at the initiative of the social workers, and that substantial elements of persuasion and value judgments were explicit, at least to the extent of openly approving or disapproving behaviour and strongly suggesting changes. This advice was, in every case, regarded by the social workers as rooted in their friendly feelings towards their families, rather than as a professional task requiring special skills in relationship; and as there was no mention by the families of this particular advice, the emotional tone of discussions could not be assessed. Yet some skills in coping with the negative feelings of clients may well have been required if this advice was to be effective: and certainly in three families this kind of advice had been followed (James, Underwood and Vincent).

In addition to the range of helping activities described as aspects of befriending, reference must be made to the many small, practical expressions of goodwill which are not in themselves helpful, and which lie outside what is normally regarded as essential to meeting clients' needs or to assisting in the solution of their problems. These expressions of goodwill exemplify the quality of relationships which many clients found supportive, yet cannot be included in any table of helpful activities: for example, calling in for a cup of tea, accepting an invitation to a party, sending cards while on holiday, extending a home-visit to play with the children, talking about one's own life and difficulties. As most families were visited weekly throughout their contact with the Unit, there was a high possibility of developing this kind of close relationship, often virtually indistinguishable from friendship; the agency's traditions of work, and the opinions of the workers that befriending was the normal context for offering help, increased the likelihood of this development. Moreover, as some clients (perhaps with good reason) resisted serious discussion of emotional difficulties within the family and avoided those elements of self-revelation or emotional dependence implicit in more intensive therapy, simple continuing friendliness was sometimes the only means by which workers could maintain contact. For example, such friendliness was the way in which the caseworker offered to Mrs James, living in a situation of chronically repetitive material and emotional needs, a sense of coherence in what would otherwise have been a fragmented series of interventions. But even among those families where more intensive discussions of feelings were acceptable, there was some awareness expressed by both clients and workers of movement back and forth between intermittent and highlighted experiences of professional modes of help and the continuing background of low-key friendly discussions and activities.

How did the families describe these intermittent experiences of professional help with feelings? Several clients, especially those referred in situations of marital conflict or depression, or who experienced serious emotional problems during the period of contact, were able to describe their increased ability to cope with difficulties by means of changes in their own attitudes and feelings; but, as we would expect, all respondents found difficulty in defining *how* these changes had occurred. For Mrs Charles and Mrs Osborne, the effect was seen in almost magical terms: both had learned to cope but remained emotionally very dependent on their social workers, and both regarded the workers' private telephone numbers as a talisman against the return of ill-fortune. Mrs Price described the mechanics of attitude-change as 'I used to blow my top with her, and she used to help me sort it out'. Similarly, Mr and Mrs Bailey: 'If my husband and I had a disagreement—they don't just listen to *one* side, they listen to *both* of you, and talk to you and try to bring you together. I know that if it had not been for Jill [the FSU worker], my husband and I would have been parted some time back, wouldn't we? I've always been the one to 'phone up, and they have come and spoken. And before they have left we have been calm, and felt as if we had acted like overgrown kids.' Mrs Sanders said of her favourite social worker, 'She'd *sit down*. And she'd take the trouble to find out what was the matter with you. She was very—interested.' Mrs Ilson spoke of her young daughter's death in a street accident outside her front door: 'It was Carole [the FSU worker] who helped me—she *wanted* to be with me, and she was there at my command. She shared all our troubles with us. She was hurt as well. She felt it as much as I felt it. If she hadn't been here, I don't know what would have happened —I think I'd have just gone mad. But she helped us to carry on. She really pulled us through.'

Bearing in mind the emphasis on friendliness and equality in relationships, the wide range of services extending well beyond the referral situation and widely varied in response to the needs of clients and the discretion of workers, it may seem surprising that four husbands avoided all contact with the social workers, and the workers felt they had failed in their work with these men. It is of course true that the families did not in every case receive *all* they asked for; limits were sometimes set upon the extent of help given, and demands, limits or structures were sometimes imposed on clients. (These issues will be considered in the following chapter, when the clients' experiences of casework relationships are more closely examined.) But these four men had sometimes strenuously avoided contact or involvement from the start of work; their avoidance was not a reaction against the limits set subsequently by the social workers. Mr Harris died before this study was made, but was well remembered for his physical violence and anger towards the social workers. His widow said: 'He's chased them out many a time. He used to say, "They're not coming dictating over me over the bloody money. We'd be better off without them." But I've always found them all right.' Mr James was usually present in interviews—and also during the research interview—but seldom said anything, and tended to speak aggressively when he did so. Mr Price avoided all contact with his wife's social worker, and the pair continued to suffer chronic marital tensions. Yet he always greeted the social worker warmly when they passed each other on the doorstep; and when he knew she was leaving her work with the Unit, he (with his wife) arranged a fish-and-chips and beer supper at their house for the social worker and her husband. The evening went well. More negatively, Mr Clark refused to discuss his marital difficulties, and resentment of the social worker sometimes led to his physical violence against his wife. Yet, according to his wife: 'He liked Pam, but he didn't like what she was. When he met her, he was ever so friendly towards her. But I think it was because of my mother—he didn't like my mother. He said I was getting like her because I'd been in touch with these people [the Unit]. I didn't think he liked that at all. I think he wanted me to have just him and nobody else.'

One common factor in these negative responses was the apparent insistence of all four on their dominance in the home. While the work of the Unit is generally based on home-visits, one wonders whether another location would have been preferable for these men. The views of their wives and of the social workers suggest that Unit House would not have been acceptable. An alternative—at least to get started—might have been a pub or club: this would, at least in some neighbourhoods, have implications for choosing the sex of the worker. (Only Mr Harris's visitor was a man.) Possibly the sex and age of the social workers may be more generally influential in such situations than is commonly thought, and may merit further study.

But Mr Harris's and Mr Clark's reactions suggest a further complexity: any kind of help, however friendly in intention and execution, implies (or is perceived to imply) some acceptance by the receiver of his dependence on the giver. Moreover, discussion of marital tensions inevitably involves some self-revelation and frequently some skill on the part of the social worker in promoting and clarifying the expression of feelings—skill which introduces the intermittent elements of professionalism to which reference has already been made, irrespective of any general context of friendliness which may successfully be created by the worker. Neither at the Sheffield Unit nor in most other agencies has particular account been taken of all these factors in considering the problems of men who need to exercise an uncompromising dominance in their personal affairs and who are perhaps too often written off as unco-operative. The generally friendly tenor of FSU work serves to emphasize their isolation from help, and the need for more imagination in reaching those for whom, in spite of their dominance, marriage and family life lack satisfaction and who seem to be irredeemably stuck in the no-man's-land between increasing their own (and others') happiness and cutting their losses by walking out.

The most helpful form of help

An attempt was made to obtain the views of families about the kinds of help which they most valued. Families were asked two questions: which kind of help had been most helpful, and—at a later point in the interview—for which problems they would refer other families to the Unit for help. In regard to this second question, answers have been compared with the families' recollections of their own primary referral problems. The results are set out in Table 8.

There seems to be a close similarity between the problems for which families were referred and the kinds of problems they

TABLE 8 *The most helpful form of help*

Family	Clients' view of the most helpful help	Problems they would refer to the Unit	Was family's problem similar to problems they would refer?
Abbott	debt-collecting	debts	yes
Bailey	debt-collecting	debts	yes
Cooper	budgeting	financial problems	yes
Charles	reliability of emotional support	emotional difficulties	yes
Dell	negotiating	'serious problems'	infer yes
Dimmock	budgeting	financial problems	yes
Ewart	friendship	material needs	yes
Francis	emotional support	material needs of children	yes
Gordon	rehousing	'all sorts'	
Harris	material aid/budgeting	material needs	yes
Ilson	emotional support	marriage problems	? yes
James	negotiating	material needs	yes
Kennedy	(husband) material aid (wife) emotional support	material needs	? yes
Lowe	negotiating	marital and emotional problems	related
Milward	negotiating	financial and material need	yes
Norris	reliability in crisis	would not refer*	
Osborne	emotional support	family emotional problems	yes
Price	emotional support	financial management	no
Roberts	support to children	material aid	yes
Sanders	emotional support	marital and financial	yes
Sheldon	loans and budgeting	'all sorts'	
Stocks	reliability in crisis	serious family problems	? yes
Tyson	emotional support	material aid	partly
Underwood	emotional support	financial marital	no yes
Vincent	sociable conversation friendship	material needs marital/wife coming alone	yes partly
Yates	emotional support	financial motherless families	yes no†

* this family said that 'it's not our place to recommend people to the Unit'; but see p. 57.
† an unexpected response, considering Mrs Yates's difficulties in relating to men.

selected as relevant to the referral of other families. Interestingly, this seems to hold good even when in their own experiences a different kind of help has become more appreciated than the help they originally sought: i.e. in the replies of the Ewart, Francis, Lowe, Roberts, Tyson, Vincent and Yates families. Mrs Price, Mrs Underwood and Mrs Yates (all unsupported women in one way or another) were the only clients to suggest problems other than their own primary referral-problems as appropriate to the Unit's work, and in none does this change appear to be based on personal experiences.

In all, fourteen families have referred twenty-one other families for the Unit's help (see Table 9). The referrals made by Mr and Mrs Norris are bewildering in view of the emphatic way they said that it was not their place to make referrals. The high rate of referral of other families is presumably indicative of the regard in which the Unit's work is held. It was noted earlier that five of the families in the study were themselves referred by family or friends. In all, five families were second-generation clients of the Unit.

Further comparisons were made to see how far the clients' perceptions of the most helpful kind of help matched both the workers' expectations of the clients' views and the workers' personal perceptions of their most valuable work with individual

TABLE 9 *Families who have referred other families*

(a) The following families informed the interviewer

Family	Problem referred	Consistent with referral intention	Similar to own problem
Abbott	debts and marital	yes	? yes
Bailey	debts	yes	yes
Gordon (3)	material needs	yes	? yes
Lowe	marital conflict	yes	related
Tyson	material aid	yes	partly
Underwood (2)	debts and money problems	yes	no
	marital	yes	yes
Vincent (3)	material needs	yes	yes
Williams (2)	marital problem deserted wife	} yes	partly

(b) The following families did not inform the interviewer

Family	Problem referred	Consistent with referral intention	Similar to own problem
Charles	parents' neglect of children	? no	no
Dell	material aid	?	yes
Harris	homeless unmarried mother	no	no
Norris (2)	help to husband while wife in ill-health	no	? yes
	a geriatric referral	no	no
Stocks	material aid	?	? yes
Ilson	mother neglecting home and in need of contraceptive advice	? yes	? yes

families. It will be seen in Table 10 that expectations and perceptions were congruent in eighteen cases; in seven others, the social workers have mistakenly assumed an identity between their own and their clients' views; in one case (Dimmock), worker's and clients' perceptions were more congruent than the worker realized; and in the final case (Tyson), the worker was not sure which aspect of help had been most valuable to the family.

Comparing these findings with those of Mayer and Timms, the degree of congruence seems remarkably high, and supports the views expressed earlier about the friendly intimacy of relationships between workers and clients and the extent to which clients' views of the help they need are respected within the scope of the help provided. At the same time (as we have suggested in relation to workers' and clients' perceptions of the referral situations), there tends to be a drifting-apart, over time, in the *quality* of these two perceptions: clients tend to recall in vivid detail a more narrowly limited aspect of the total situation, while workers tend to make broader generalizations. It was discovered further that, in seven cases, the most recent worker did not know, or had wrongly remembered, the name of the beginning worker. In five cases, clients' initial expectations of the Unit's attitudes were inaccurately recalled or inferred. The most recent workers with six families were unaware that they had referred (in all) eleven 'new' families to the Unit. And in Table 10 it was shown that

TABLE 10 *A comparison of workers' and families' perceptions of the most effective help*

	Client's view	Worker's expectations of client's view	Worker's own view
Abbott	debt collecting	befriending	befriending
Bailey	debt collecting	emotional support	emotional support
Cooper	budgeting	budgeting	budgeting
Charles	reliability of emotional support	befriending	befriending
Dell	negotiating with agencies	emotional support	emotional support
Dimmock	budgeting	emotional support	budgeting
Ewart	befriending	befriending	emotional support
Francis	emotional support	emotional support	emotional support
Gordon	rehousing and reliability	rehousing	rehousing
Harris	material aid and budgeting	budgeting	budgeting
Ilson	emotional support	emotional support	emotional support
James	negotiating debts	material aid	material aid
Kennedy	(husband) material aid (wife) emotional support	material aid	emotional support
Lowe	negotiating	material aid	material aid
Milward	negotiating	negotiating	negotiating
Norris	reliability in crisis	material aid	material aid
Osborne	emotional support	emotional support	emotional support
Price	emotional support	emotional support	emotional support
Roberts	support to children	emotional support	emotional support
Sanders	emotional support	emotional support	emotional support
Sheldon	loans and budgeting	budgeting	budgeting
Stocks	reliability in crisis	emotional support	emotional support
Tyson	emotional support	not sure	not sure
Underwood	emotional support	emotional support	emotional support
Vincent	sociable conversation	budgeting	guidance on children
Williams	befriending	emotional support	emotional support
Yates	emotional support	befriending	befriending

seven workers had mistakenly assumed an identity between their own and clients' views concerning the most helpful kind of help employed. As our impression was of a high degree of identification between clients and workers in the Unit, we must assume that wider and possibly more critical discrepancies would be found in the work of some other services. Mayer and Timms have explored aspects of these discrepancies in a voluntary service from which dissatisfied clients could escape. It would be instructive to explore what happens to process and relationship in social work when dissatisfied clients are, in one sense or another, captive.

Finally, in considering the help most valued by clients, an attempt was made to estimate how far their comments reflected a shift in opinion since the beginning of contact with the Unit—movement based upon experience of the Unit's work, and also possibly upon identification with the professional thinking and methods of their caseworkers. My assumption was that satisfaction/dissatisfaction and outcome (assessed in terms of social functioning) would be related in some way; and that mutual satisfaction would be associated with an increasing identity between the values of worker and client (values expressed in terms of relationship, or in terms of purpose).

In most cases, no major change was recorded in clients' opinions about the most helpful mode of help. In the following eight families, however, some changes had occurred as recorded by the clients:

Mr and Mrs Ewart: material aid and negotiation remained important to them, but they had come to value most the worker's friendship.

Mr and Mrs Francis: a similar shift towards the appreciation of the worker's emotional support.

Mrs Gordon: a shift of concern from material aid towards the supportive value of the mothers' group (see earlier quotation).

Mrs Ilson: from material aid to a special appreciation of the support received when her daughter died.

Mrs Kennedy: from material aid to an emphasis on emotional support in her feelings of depression.

Mrs Tyson: a similar shift from material aid to emotional support.

Mr and Mrs Vincent: from material aid to an emphasis on equal conversation and the 'sociability' of the worker.

Mr and Mrs Williams: from material aid to a special appreciation of the emotional support and moral goodness of one worker, who gave up time and energy in helping Mr Williams to get on his feet following discharge from prison.

It is interesting to note that all these families except Francis and Tyson began their association with the Unit in fear or hostility.

No conclusion can be drawn concerning any relationship between a shift of opinion and a feeling of satisfaction with the Unit's work. These clients were satisfied, but so were virtually all the others. It is possible, however, that a relationship exists between this shift of opinion and improvements in social functioning. Conclusions here can be no more than tentative, but in general the social performance of most of these families appears to have improved to a greater degree than the average social performance of the group as a whole.

Workers were asked to compare each family's situation now and at referral in relation to the following eight areas:

(1) financial management;
(2) marital relationships;
(3) parent-child relationships;
(4) husband's work attendance;
(5) children's general social behaviour;
(6) the individual role competence (as parent and spouse) of each partner;
(7) capacities to cope with inner feelings of distress;
(8) capacities to cope with external unexpected pressures.

The workers' replies were recorded in each area on the scale 'better/the same/worse'.

The Ewart family showed improvement in the behaviour of the children, but not elsewhere. There had been no deterioration of performance, but no positive changes either. They were, however, an exception in this small group. The other families may be scaled as in Table 11. Five families in the group seem to have been helped to cope with feelings of distress and panic; financial management has improved in five cases, and marital relationships in six. On

TABLE 11 *Perceived changes in social functioning (1)*

Family	Areas improved	Areas the same	Areas worse	No change required
Francis	1, 2, 4, 6, 7, 8	3, 5		
(work with the husband had been especially effective and co-operative)				
Gordon	1, 2, 3, 6, 7, 8			4, 5
Ilson	2, 3, 5, 6, 7, 8			1, 4
Kennedy	1, 2, 6, 7, 8	3, 4		5
Tyson	3	6, 7, 8		1, 2, 4, 5
Vincent	1, 2, 3, 5, 6, 8	7	4	
Williams	1, 2, 4, 5, 6, 7	8		3

the whole, these findings compare favourably with those for the other families recorded in Chapter 7.

It would be rash to assume that these improvements are wholly the results of social work help, but equally the possible influences of the social workers cannot be ignored. Whether these improvements are attributable to the development of common values in relationships or to the discovery of a common purpose of working together cannot be said with certainty. Possibly the mixture is different in each case. It is likely that a working partnership and sense of common purpose developed between the social worker and Mr and Mrs Francis, and with Mrs Gordon. This may be true also of Mrs Tyson, with whom the social worker did not enjoy a particularly close relationship but who, in the research interview, described her own voluntary social work for a local pre-school play group; she had clearly adopted some of the work values of social workers. In the other families, I was made aware of clients' identification with the relationship-values of the social workers rather than with their functional purposes. Mrs Ilson became particularly animated in describing the caseworker's empathetic relationship with her at the time of her daughter's death; Mrs Kennedy's best safeguard against depression was a personal identification with the caseworker; Mr and Mrs Vincent spoke at length about the importance of equality in relationships, identified themselves with students (their favourite caseworker left them to become a student), and emphasized conversation and sociability as the greatest benefit they received from the Unit; Mr and Mrs Williams were particularly impressed with the moral goodness of one caseworker, had been surprised that anyone could be so generous towards them (in moral rather than material terms), and wanted to be identified with him as a person.

Notes

The complexity of distinguishing between the actual help received and the relationships of the social workers is well illustrated by McKay *et al.* (1973) in their study of clients' satisfactions and dissatisfactions in a Social Services Department. 'Although we tried to differentiate between the consumers' attitudes towards the department, the services received and their individual worker, it proved difficult to achieve. Consumers who expressed negative attitudes towards their social workers were more likely to be dissatisfied.... Help received made little difference to whether the social workers were easy to talk to or good listeners.... Only a few social workers mentioned ... the personal relationship between worker and client as something the majority of clients appreciated, yet nearly all clients appreciated the visits and liked their social workers.' These comments support the (at the time) surprising degree of satisfaction expressed by the Unit's clients, and the difficulties, shortly to be described, of distinguishing between help and relationship.

5
Memories of the duration of contact in relation to the families' preferences for particular social workers

An hour spent with one person may seem much shorter than an hour; with another it may feel like an age. Two people, while apparently of equal importance to another person at one time, may later be remembered differently: one vividly, the other hardly at all. The next chapter will be concerned with the opinions of clients concerning their relationships with the social workers. The present chapter will draw attention to two indicators, less clear-cut than expressed opinions, of the quality of relationships: clients' and workers' impressions of the length of contact; and the relationship between a client's preference for a particular social worker and that worker's place in a series of workers.

Recollections and impressions of the length of contact between families and the Unit are set out in detail in Appendix V. Briefly, nine families accurately recollected the length of contact, three offered underestimations of up to twelve months, while five overestimated the period by between seven and twelve months, and eight overestimated the period by more than a year. (Two respondents were wholly unable to estimate the period.) Among the social workers, thirteen accurately estimated the length of contact between family and Unit, but ten social workers (compared with three clients) underestimated this period, while four (compared with thirteen clients) made overestimations. A summary of the findings is set out in Table 12. In broad terms, social workers tended more frequently to underestimate and clients to overestimate the period of working together, and clients' overestimations tend to be considerable ones. Among these, the length of contact with social workers for whom clients felt affection or dependence was the most usually exaggerated. It is interesting that three women without husbands, whose effective contact had been with one worker only, overestimated this length of time very considerably.

TABLE 12 *Recollections of the length of contact (summary)*

	Underestimates (months)			Accurate	Overestimates (months)			Don't know
	13+	7–12	1–6		1–6	7–12	13+	
Clients	0	1	2	9	0	5	8	2
Social workers	1	4	5	13	0	4	0	0

Among social workers, exaggeration of the length of contact was associated most with their finding a particular family emotionally demanding. There was no relationship between the under- and overestimations of social workers and clients. In general—although this is not set out in the tables—it was found that clients' memories of the names, and order of appearance, of their social workers were more reliable than the recollections of the social workers.

Families were also asked to nominate one worker, if possible, as their favourite. The purpose of this, discussed in the following chapter, was to assist them in identifying the characteristics which they associated with 'good' work or 'good' workers. But a consideration of this preference, when related to the length of contact of each worker and to the order of workers, gives rise to two alternative hypotheses: first, that clients tend to relate most closely to the caseworkers either who initiate the contact or who are most recently in touch; second, that clients tend to relate most closely, in a succession of workers, to the one with whom they have had the longest relationship. The evidence for these hypotheses is set out in Table 13. No conclusion may be drawn from the first twelve entries; but from this point alternative patterns begin to emerge. It will be noted that, of the twenty-five families who had been visited by more than one social worker/social work student, nineteen expressed a preference.

From a consideration of the replies of the thirteen who not only expressed a preference for a particular social worker but also had some scope for the exercise of choice, it will be seen that seven nominated the most recent worker; in six cases, this happened to be the worker with whom they had had the longest association. Four families nominated the first worker, who in three instances had also been in touch with them longest (the Lowe family overestimated the period spent with the first worker, whose actual length of contact was equal to another's). Two families nominated workers with whom they had been in touch longest, but who were neither their first nor their most recent visitors.

TABLE 13 *The sequential position of the preferred worker*

Family	No. of	Was preference expressed	Position of preferred worker	Had preferred worker the longest contact?
Dell	1	not applicable	—	—
Tyson	1	not applicable	—	—
Cooper	1+1 st.	yes	first/continuing	yes
Price	1+2 sts	yes	first/continuing	yes
Abbott	2	no	not applicable	not applicable
Dimmock	2	yes	first	(equal) yes
Stocks	2	yes	first	no
Underwood	2	yes	last	yes
James	2+1 st.	no	not applicable	not applicable
Sanders	2+1 st.	yes	first	no
Ewart	2+2 sts	no	not applicable	not applicable
Charles	2+2 sts	no	not applicable	not applicable
Ilson	2+2 sts	yes	last	yes
Roberts	2+2 sts	yes	last	yes
Vincent	2+2 sts	yes	last	yes
Gordon	2+3 sts	yes	first	no
Kennedy	2+3 sts	yes (wife only)	last	yes
Francis	2+4 sts	yes (wife only)	last	yes
Harris	2+5 sts	yes (student)	last	no
Norris	3+1 st.	yes	middle	yes
Sheldon	3+1 st.	yes	first	yes
Williams	3+1 st.	yes (student)	middle	yes
Lowe	3+1 st.	yes	middle	(equal) yes
Bailey	3+2 sts	no	not applicable	not applicable
Osborne	4	no	not applicable	not applicable
Yates	4	yes	last	yes
Milward	5+3 sts	yes	first	yes

In this table, 'st.'=student. Students' work is undertaken in the context of a social worker's continuing contact with the family. Thus, '1+1 st.' implies the sequence worker-student-return of first worker; '1+2 sts' implies the sequence worker-student-return of first worker-second student-return of first worker; '2+2 sts' most usually implies the sequence first worker-first student-first worker-second worker-second student-second worker. (It will be recalled that in the selection of families it was decided to avoid those whose most recent contact had been with a student. This was achieved, save in the case of Mrs Harris whose social worker had not re-established regular contact following the departure of the most recent student.)

The numbers are too small for firm conclusions to be drawn from the material presented in this chapter. It seems likely, however, that some special regard is accorded by clients to the social workers they meet at the initial crisis of referral, and to those with whom they are most recently in touch. The choice depends perhaps on the length of contact in each case. Although students were often mentioned with approval, only in one case was a student selected as the favourite worker; this is probably because of the relative brevity of their contact. At the same time, the length of contact may be extended or reduced in the perception of both workers and clients. It sometimes happens that a close or dependent relationship is exaggerated in the memory of the client.

Families' preferences for particular social workers, and their reasons

All families spoke warmly of most of the Unit workers they had met. Only four expressed any serious dislikes (one each), and three of these were of students. Among the social workers, interest in each other's families was considerable; and in some respects, at the time of this study, the Unit itself functioned as a family might do. Informal discussions of each other's work took place as a matter of course; workers and students lunched together, and several families during the research interviews mentioned having tea, coffee or a make-shift meal with the social workers when they visited the Unit, particularly at times of urgent difficulty. Some families felt, therefore, that they had friendly relationships with several social workers other than the worker specifically assigned to them. At the end of a research interview it was not unusual for enquiries to be made about the whereabouts and well-being of past and present workers and students, some of whom had been encountered informally in the kitchen at Unit House. Some families were described to me as 'Unit families', in that the family network and the Unit's near-familial network interwove at several points, and considerable goodwill flowed spontaneously (and unrecorded) in both directions. Generally, when clients expressed no preference for a particular worker, they simply meant that they liked them all. A few clients spontaneously described the Unit as 'closer than family' or 'closer than neighbours'. Six families expressed no preferences among the workers they had known (Abbott, Bailey, Charles, Ewart, James, Osborne); two others had been in touch with only one social worker and were unable to express a preference. With regard to the preferences of the remaining nineteen, the most recent worker was able to guess these accurately in thirteen instances.

The six families whose preferences were not guessed accurately provide a useful preliminary indication of those aspects of relationship which the families generally regarded as important, but which are sometimes overlooked when the effectiveness of social services is considered. In the case of Mr and Mrs Gordon, the social worker guessed that they would prefer the colleague who had made the closest relationship with the husband; but they chose instead the social worker who had helped Mrs Gordon to feel relaxed and not humiliated in asking for help. Mrs Harris was thought to have no preferences, but named a student with whom she identified herself as a young unmarried woman. It was believed that Mr and Mrs James preferred a social worker who had been 'very successful and efficient' in obtaining material and financial assistance from a variety of sources at a time of crisis; but they spoke instead of a particularly patient social worker with whom they felt comfortable and who made long home-visits. Similarly, Mrs Lowe preferred a 'homely' social worker, whom she identified as 'better than a neighbour', to a more efficient provider of material aid. Mr and Mrs Sanders preferred a young worker whom they regarded as like themselves, rather than the older social worker with whom they readily discussed their marital problems. Mr and Mrs Sheldon did not choose the worker with whom they had effectively worked out many problems over a long period, but one whom they regarded as outstandingly good in moral terms—generous and keeping confidences entirely to himself.

When the social workers accurately guessed their clients' preferences, the reasons for the preferences were in all but four instances accurately guessed as well. In these four cases, the social workers assumed that preference would be based on material aid or the efficient provision of other help related to financial welfare. The families selected instead more intangible ethical considerations: gentleness (Ewart), emotional reliability (Kennedy), patience (Stocks), goodness (Williams). The numbers are small, but it appears that the social workers placed more weight than the clients on efficiency and speed in practical matters. Clients spoke more readily —and often at length—about qualities of personal relationships than about the workers' activities.

Finally, the reasons given—all in all—for the clients' preferences for particular workers were as indicated in Table 14; the number of times in which a particular quality was given first place is indicated in brackets. The social workers were also asked which, in their view, had been the most successful worker with each family. It is worth noting that in all save three cases they identified the workers for whom clients had expressed their preferences —preferences which, as we have seen, were based primarily on qualities of relationship rather than of action.

Finally, a comment about 'Unit families'. It was not the purpose of this study to evaluate the work of the Unit, and no information was directly sought to show whether (and how) changes of worker mattered to the families. Some families were described by the social

TABLE 14 *Reasons for clients' preferences*

Informality*, homely, easy to talk to (5)
Understanding why the client cannot always tell the truth; getting close enough for honesty (4)
Patience in listening (3)
Keeping confidences (3)
Ability to take control (physically and/or emotionally) when client is at his wits' end (3)
Morally very good, 'not riff-raff' (3)
Dependability (2)
Caring about everybody in the family (2)
Politeness and appropriate formality* (1)

* The same social worker was praised by two families for his formality and informality. The approach to each—judged from the records—had been deliberate and calculated, and may provide us with consumer views of the difference between professional help and befriending.

workers as having made a relationship with the whole Unit, rather than with just one worker, the assumption being that in such cases a change of worker would not be experienced adversely. The change of workers arose spontaneously, however, in interviews with Mrs Harris, Mrs Sheldon and Mrs Yates. Mrs Sheldon and Mrs Yates said that they would have preferred to have just one social worker, 'but we didn't mind because everyone was nice; they've all been sociable and helpful'. Mrs Harris described a recent student, of whom she was very fond, and said she was glad she had left because she felt too close to her. Parting would have become more difficult the longer the student stayed. But, she said, 'it's really nice to see different faces ... because, you know, if you see one face all the time, you get fed up with *that*! So they change hands, so that, if one can't come, then another can.'

Notes

Reference should be made to Mayer and Timms (1970, pp. 107-10) on social workers' attitudes most closely associated with the clients' satisfaction with casework help. Here also, emphasis is placed on the worker's personal acceptability, his concern and activity, his trust, his ability to lessen feelings of shame in seeking help, and material aid. The present study supports their findings that clients perceive 'successful' working relationships as friendship, and seek a reciprocal relationship of 'repaying' the social workers, but out of friendliness rather than obligation.

6
Relationships between families and social workers

Mayer and Timms (1970) have suggested that working-class clients see the caseworker's relationship not as professional, in the sense of being limited by requirements of treatment or social role, but as personal, friendly, and broadly involved in day-to-day concerns. Our findings lend support to this view. Though the reluctance of being a client and the fears of interference which these authors have documented may not always abate, they appear to be offset by workers possessing particular qualities of personality. Mayer and Timms speak of clients' responsiveness to a worker's interest, activity, trust, and ability to reduce feelings of shame; the examples they give are matched by the comments of clients in the present study. It will be apparent from this study that the predominant style of work at the FSU is more nearly akin to supportive-directive help than to insight therapy. It has not therefore been possible to compare clients' perceptions of these two modes of helping, as was done in the FWA study where both modes were employed and were regarded as alternative rather than compatible. The compatibility of these modes in some family situations has been suggested in the section on the scope of help offered to the families. We are aware, however, that 'insight therapy' is variously defined by social workers, and, for lack of adequate and precise observation of what actually goes on in the Unit's casework relationships, we cannot be sure that the 'professional' help to which we have referred earlier is comparable with 'insight therapy'.

At the same time, it does appear that the compatibility of 'supportive-directive' help with the families' views of their needs did in some cases facilitate the development of a relationship within which professionally more sophisticated forms of help—help with feelings, attitudes and responses—became possible; and that this help was not always incompatible with intimacy in relationships (in particular, with clients' knowledge of some parts of the workers' private lives). The mixing of friendliness and professional task is illustrated by the clients' approval of the workers' occasional exercise of authority and power over them, irrespective of an underlying relationship of mutual intimacy. Kadushin (1972) has suggested that social workers may properly share their own pertinent life experiences with their clients as an aid to social learning and to the clients' identification with certain values and goals. In such cases, however, where intimacy and a professional relationship are deemed to be compatible, success in achieving a balance between the two components, relevant to the needs and concerns both of client and agency, depends on the professional discretion and wisdom of the social worker. The intuitions of friendship may be insufficient, as will be shown by the comments of one client for whom information about the social worker's life was an impediment rather than a help.

In relation to this general topic, reference should be made to the later chapter dealing with the social workers' descriptions of 'good' and 'successful' practice. In general, 'good' casework appeared to be related by the workers to their emotional and ethical input; and, in some definitions of the terms employed, a cognitive divorce was implied between this input and the outcome of work perceived in terms of social functioning. Where such a divorce exists, a further aspect of the worker's professional integrity must be his preparedness to explore how far his ethical input (of acceptance, for example) is compatible with the achievement by clients of socially acceptable or essential standards of behaviour. Again, a worker may be so concerned to win his client's acceptance as to collude with socially or ethically unacceptable behaviour. I have no reason to suppose that the workers in this study ran into such difficulties, but the findings suggest that potential difficulties of these kinds may arise when professional relationships cease to be regarded as essentially separate from and alternative to friendship.

Intimacy and sharing in relationships implies two further issues, one unfashionable and one fashionable. The first of these concerns how far social workers may be regarded, in Halmos's words (1965), as the 'moral tutors' of their clients; and the second concerns the notion of participation in welfare. On the first of these, the evidence suggests that the families' acceptance of their social workers depended in large part on the workers *not* giving advice; as noted earlier, several clients will be quoted to suggest that they draw a clear distinction between suggesting and advising—a distinction based on relevance and on attitude rather than on factual or verbal content. Yet advice-giving—however described or perceived—was mentioned by the social workers as one of their functions, and there is ample evidence to show that direct advice was given in many situations, accompanied by moral or emotional pressure. In a few instances, moreover, clients appear not only to have followed advice but to have identified with the value- or functional-orientations of their social workers. It will be suggested that this tutelage was acceptable principally because of its context of partnership, intimacy and sharing in relationships.

With regard to the second issue, participation in welfare, one respondent stressed equality and sociability as the most influential aspects of the social worker's relationship with himself and his wife. Another—as we have seen—emphasized the participatory helping processes of the mothers' group. Furthermore, it will be shown that several families have given financial help to the Unit as tokens of their participation. Pinker (1971) suggests that for most people participant citizenship has very little meaning, that most applicants to social services are 'paupers at heart', and that the achievement of democratic participation will depend on the extent to which clients attain a lively experience of sharing in the processes of service. I shall suggest, through reference to the comments of the families, that this experience was present in many worker-client relationships, and that—where it is present—two kinds of outcome seem to be inevitable: first, that the perceptions among participants of the roles of clients and workers differ in some respects (but not entirely) from those associated with traditional norms of casework relationships; and, second, that 'the habit of deference and gratitude'—though still untouched—sometimes gives way to the expression of short-lived hostility.

In order to provide a framework for the presentation of material concerning the quality and content of worker-client relationships, evidence will be grouped under the following four headings: the clients' feelings for their current or most recent social workers; the use made by the workers of their own personal disclosures; the use of authority and the setting of limits; the clients' perceptions of the attitudes of preferred workers. Following this, there will be a comment on relationships in terms of the roles of workers and clients. The overall intention of this chapter is to consider the extent to which a common basis of relationship exists, upon which professional forms of help and help through befriending may both be built and utilized in accordance with a client's current and changing needs.

The clients' feelings for their most recent social workers

Most of this chapter is concerned with the investments that social workers make in their relationships with clients. During the research interviews with the families, both at the time and especially when listening to the tape-recordings afterwards, an attempt was made to assess the quality of clients' investment in relationships with social workers. No precise means of assessment were available, but direct verbal indications were sought of the presence of three feelings towards the social worker:

goodwill
: i.e. not wishing him harm, expressing at least a passing interest in his well-being, not wishing strongly that he would stop visiting;

confidence
: i.e. belief that the social worker has the family's well-being at heart; belief that he will respect confidential information;

affection
: i.e. warm regard, wanting to do something to help the worker, feeling concern for the worker's happiness in his private life.

Subsequently, in interviews with the social workers, the question was asked, in respect of each family, whether the worker felt he had the clients' goodwill, confidence or affection, and the words or actions by which these feelings were shown.

The comparative results are set out in Table 15 by means of plus signs. Evidence gained directly from research interviews with families is recorded first in each column; the social workers' opinions are recorded second, in brackets. Where no plus sign is recorded, this shows that this particular feeling was not indicated by what the clients said in interview, or that the social workers considered this feeling to be absent from the relationship. Where the feeling content of relationships differed with wife and husband, this is indicated by w and H respectively.

The indications are that the families expressed goodwill in all save three cases. A high degree of confidence was indicated by sixteen families, and affection by at least six. It seems possible—though the small numbers prevent more than a very tentative impression—that the social workers felt less certainty of the confidence of their clients than the clients professed in interview; but, on the other hand, they experienced some affection from six clients whose feelings were not so certainly apparent in the research interviews.

How were these feelings expressed? The following indicators were mentioned by the social workers:

(1) verbally: there were eight instances of clients' telling the worker how they felt about him or her in a natural and relaxed way, and ten instances of clients being more honest and open about themselves (including serious negative factors) than the needs of the case required;

(2) by actions on behalf of the social worker: nine instances of

TABLE 15 *Clients' feelings for the most recent social workers*

Family	Goodwill	Confidence	Affection
Abbott	+(+)	+(+)	W(W)
Bailey	+(+)	+(+)	( )
Cooper	+(+)	+(+)	+( )
Charles	+(+)	+(+)	+(+)
Dell	+( )	(+)	( )
Dimmock	+(+)	+(+)	( )
Ewart	+(+)	+(+)	+(+)
Francis	+(+)	W(W)	W(W)
Gordon	+(+)	+(+)	W(+)
Harris	+(+)	+(+)	+(+)
Ilson	+(+)	+(+)	+(+)
James	W(W)	W(W)	( )
Kennedy	+(+)	W(+)	(W)
Lowe	+(+)	+(+)	
Milward	+(+)	W(W)	(W)
Norris	+(+)	( )	( )
Osborne	+(+)	+(+)	+(+)
Price	+(+)	+(+)	W(W)
Roberts	+(+)	+(+)	(H)
Sanders	+(+)	+(+)	W( )
Sheldon	+(+)	+( )	(W)
Stocks	+(+)	+(+)	( )
Tyson	+(+)	+( )	( )
Underwood	W(W)	W(W)	( )
Vincent	+(+)	+( )	(+)
Williams	+(+)	+( )	(+)
Yates	+(+)	+(+)	( )

running errands (unasked) on the worker's behalf, twelve of writing him friendly letters, giving presents, showing concern for the worker's own family, and three of maintaining debt payments over long periods when the worker was unable to visit;

(3) by generosity to the Unit: two instances of paying more for the clothes received than the Unit asked for, two of giving personal service to the Unit, and three of giving money to the Unit out of small wins on the football pools. (An earlier note has shown the extent to which families also referred others to the Unit, possibly indicating goodwill towards both.)

In addition to the three families who shared their pools winnings, a further six spontaneously mentioned in interview that they would give money to the Unit if they were lucky in this way, and I have no reason to doubt their sincerity. Two mothers said that, when their children were older, they would help the Unit as unpaid cleaners.

We were unable to establish any connection between the presence of these warm and generous feelings and any special or unusual help from the social workers. Neither was there an indication that these feelings represented a need to repay, a need to buy one's way out of a feeling of moral obligation. Mrs Gordon and Mrs Ilson, typically, felt warmly towards the Unit precisely because they no longer experienced this kind of obligation nor felt humiliated by receiving help; and Mr Vincent's goodwill was based, he said, on the replacement of obligation by equality in relationship. No association can be made either—as will be apparent in the next chapter—between these feelings and achievements in the families' social functioning.

The only suggestions that can be drawn from the evidence are these. First, that this emotional investment by many clients was a response to the generation of friendly feelings by the social workers, and that it is to be seen as an end in itself: from the clients' viewpoint, these relationships were friendships which would continue in this way, irrespective of changes in their needs or circumstances. Thus, twelve families specifically stated that they did not wish (or had not wished) their link with the Unit to end. A further twelve said that they would have (or have had) mixed feelings about any cessation of the social workers' visits. Only three families saw this ending in clearly positive terms, representing social achievement and problem-solving on their own part. (Details of these findings are included in the next chapter.)

Second, there may be a consequential discrepancy between the clients' apparent concern—even, in some cases, preoccupation—with the goodwill element of a relationship and the social workers' hopes that clients will achieve independence from the agency and from the need for help. In other words, as we shall see, the link between notions of successful work and good work ('good' used in a moral sense) is an uncertain one, for success implies an ending to the relationship, while good work indicates the building of a relationship which, on one side at least, may be seen as a permanent one. In this case, purposefulness in social work practice tends to be related more to shared effort in immediate crises and short-term plans than to a shared longer-term goal of independent social functioning. This is not to suggest that the social workers in this study did not have this goal in mind; even less that they were lacking a sense of purpose. On the contrary, the dedicated work which we studied, and the families experienced, is explicable only in terms of a general sense of purpose rather than of limited and pragmatic problem-solving. It is, however, unlikely that this long-term purposefulness was much discussed and shared between workers and clients, or that it was comprehended in the same way by them; an accidental and unacknowledged discrepancy therefore grows at the heart of this kind of helping relationship, whereas it is less likely to grow when both sides see relationship and function in more specific and professional terms. Friendships are, by their nature, not purposive. It would be desirable, therefore, to be able to distinguish between friendship and befriending when thinking of the commitment of both sides in the helping relationship; but this is difficult ground for the perceptions of workers and clients alike.

Third, it seems that the social workers achieved an intimacy (sometimes perceived as an equality) with their clients, such that in some situations the usual role-distinctiveness of helper and helped became blurred. For example, as we have seen, some clients gave help to the Unit and the Unit's workers; Mrs Gordon was both the helper and the helped in the mothers' group. This represents an achievement in relationships not generally associated with casework practice. It is usually more canvassed (though perhaps not more frequently achieved) among community workers, and is a goal sought by those employed experimentally as 'detached' workers in various settings. The present study serves as a reminder of the complexities of this approach, relative to traditional ideas of 'a professional relationship' and 'professional purpose', and this will be considered further in the section concerned with the use of authority and the setting of limits.

The use made of the social workers' personal disclosures

This was a focus of questioning in the interviews with both families and social workers. If befriending/friendship/friendliness formed a basis of much of the Unit's work, it was to be supposed that the families would know something of the social workers' own lives. We wished to discover whether this was so, to what extent and in what areas of life, and its practical effects on the casework relationship.

Two reservations can be made, one emphasized by a client and the other by several of the social workers. The acceptability to the client of information about a social worker's life depends on its similarity and relevance to the client's own circumstances, hopes or phantasies. For example, cooking meals, going shopping, experiences on holiday, going to a dance could all be appropriate in some if not all particulars. But a young social worker telling a middle-aged, tired and over-burdened woman about her indecision concerning which boyfriend to go out with can only be annoying, especially when pursued at length. (One client had this experience with a student.) Second, the social worker needs to ration what he says about himself so that it falls within what are, to the clients, acceptable emotional limits: several workers defined these limits in terms of casual rather than close friendship, irrespective of the clients' perceptions of the actual closeness of this friendship. Nor should the disclosure change the focus of the relationship from concern with the family's needs to concern for the worker's needs, nor feed any inclination in a particular client to mis-use personal information.

Within these two reservations, it appeared that the social workers' usual practice was to disclose information when directly asked, or when it arose naturally in the course of conversation; but not to introduce it gratuitously or without relevance to the discussion in hand. This was accepted as a norm of interviewing practice, to the extent that social workers seemed to believe that they should explain to the interviewer why in some cases they were justified in withholding information about themselves, but never why they were justified in giving it. The findings showed that seventeen families knew a considerable amount about the personal circumstances and history of their social workers, while ten knew only whether a worker was married and had children, and basic information of this kind. In the view of the social workers, among the seventeen families holding considerable personal information about them, ten families had been positively helped by it, but for the other seven the information had made no detectable difference to the relationship, or to the flow or effectiveness of the casework.

The principal reasons given for the helpfulness of this information to ten families were verified both with the families concerned and with the workers; they were as follows:

that the family needed (or at least enjoyed) a feeling of shared intimacy (4);
that help was acceptable because it came from a 'real person' (3);
that this information indicated to clients whether the worker was capable of understanding their particular problems (2);
that the client was helped to cope by hearing how the worker coped with her own problems (1).

Mrs Ilson said: 'Many social workers don't say anything about themselves, and try to hide their feelings—you know, making out they're all good. But, you know—you can always tell if they're happy and sincere or not; you can tell by the look on their faces. Pat comes here sometimes, and we get to talking. She never hides anything—it gives me some idea of how to cope with my problems.'

The use of authority and the setting of limits

An impression will probably be gained of generous, warm and permissive relationships. This is accurate to a point, but may all too readily be interpreted as indicative of lack of structure in interviews and in the management of needs and resources, of the abandoning of any recognition of priorities in the use of time and resources, and of the irresponsible resignation of opportunities to offer a family guidance in ways of achieving greater enjoyments and satisfactions. Permissiveness may all too easily be perceived as, and indeed become, stagnation. Moreover, it has been suggested earlier that the relationships discussed in this study were in several cases experienced as friendships and therefore, in the clients' perceptions at least, lacking a sense of purpose extending beyond the requirements of the immediate situation.

Yet equally there have been hints in earlier chapters that these worker-client relationships were not simple friendships: material help was sometimes limited for several families; the table of categories of help showed the use of direct advice in sensitive and personal areas of living; and, in one case in particular, the social worker's concern to off-set her client's self-destructive manipulation of resources indicated a detached and professional appraisal of a complex emotional situation.

When the families were asked whether the social workers had ever said or done anything they disliked or resented, they replied, for the most part, that they had not. In the light of discussions, it seemed likely that the clients were sticking up for their (professional) friends in front of a stranger. The social workers were also asked about this, therefore, and were questioned in addition about their use of firmness and the setting of limits (on resources or in relationship), and for their assessment of the responses of the families in these unpermissive situations. The workers' replies were checked, so far as possible, against the day-to-day records of the cases involved.

Before setting out the results of this enquiry, it is necessary to clarify the ideas subsumed in the notions of firmness and limit-setting. By *firmness* was meant the exercise of definite and precise demands of the following kinds upon the manners or actions of clients:

> instructions to carry out a particular task;
> advising very strongly a particular course of action (the exercise of moral pressure);

telling clients how they ought to behave towards others, and as far as possible requiring this behaviour;

strongly discouraging certain kinds of talk (usually to children or in front of children);

refusing to give the advice demanded by clients, in those cases where clients were deemed to be competent to decide;

refusing material aid and short-term loans.

In the *setting of limits* is included

the social worker's assumption of responsibility for the shape and content of an interview, by steering discussions away from some topics and towards others;

reminding clients of their social obligations and the results of not meeting them (e.g. in paying debts and rent, and in co-operating with other agencies);

certain skilled tasks associated with the practice of casework in the sector of feelings and attitudes—in particular, accepting and containing negative feelings, avoiding collusion and resolving manipulative situations, and helping clients to resolve phantasies about themselves, their families, the social services, or the powers of the caseworker.

The clients' responses to experiences are recorded in one of three ways:

accepting these experiences in the long run (irrespective of annoyance at the time) as necessary and helpful;

continuing to resent;

uninfluenced in any way (appearing not to have taken much notice).

In broad terms, it seems that in only four families was no firmness ever employed by a social worker, and in two of these it had not been found necessary, in the view of the social workers, to set any of the limits defined here. These four were families whose demands or expectations had never been regarded by the social workers (nor noted in the records) as unreasonable, and who tended, possibly, to see the social worker essentially as a professional helper. This would seem to be borne out by reference to the earlier table of clients' feelings about their social workers where, with the exception of Mrs Osborne, little indication of affection is recorded. (Mrs Osborne's emotional difficulties—of guilt, despair and self-disgust—required not only skill in the social worker but some therapeutic use of transference in relationship.)

In sixteen cases, the social workers considered that they had occasionally said or done things which in the short term at least angered or hurt the families. Seventeen families had received strongly-worded advice at some time, and all other kinds of firmness had been variously used in more than a third of the work undertaken, including the refusal of material aid to ten families on one or more occasions.

The most frequent kinds of limiting were by controlling and steering the content of interviews (fourteen families), emphasizing the importance of paying rent or debts (seven families), and—of particular significance in view of the general friendliness of relationships—avoiding or resolving collusion with clients (twelve families).

The clients appear to have responded by acceptance in the long run in nineteen families; some continuing resentment was thought to be present in four. Clients in six families seemed to take little or no notice. (This question was hardly applicable in the Sheldon and Tyson families; in three others (Abbott, Ewart and Stocks), the responses were varied according to the areas of firmness or limiting exercised; and, in two, responses varied between husband and wife.)

In general, greater firmness appears to have been used in the 'open' cases than workers recall in the 'closed' cases. It was certainly remarkable that the refusal of material aid was not recorded in any of the 'closed' cases; this was the first area of study in which a major difference occurred between 'open' and 'closed' cases. We were not aware of any deliberate and general change in the Unit's policies of help; the differences may therefore have been related either realistically to the different needs of the families, or to differences in methods of work among more recently appointed members of staff. If the latter, then two hypotheses may be formulated from the findings:

> first, that greater firmness (increasing the emotional demands made on clients) and the setting of limits are not incompatible with close relationships, nor with the clients' identification with the relationship- or work-values of the social workers; and
> second, that, assuming a basis of close relationships, the greater exercise of firmness increases short-term but not long-term resentment.

In support of these hypotheses, comments are recorded below from six families who considered that firmness and limiting, in discussion or behaviour, had been valuable aspects of the help they received, provided that these were exercised in the context of a generally acceptable manner and—we may infer—an acceptable relationship:

Mrs Price: 'She's a good listener, a bit forceful ... Some of

TABLE 16 *Firmness and limits employed by the social workers, and the families' responses to them*

Family	Worker has sometimes offended family	Firmness						Setting limits								Response		
		1	2	3	4	5	6	7	8	9	10	11	12	13	14	A	R	N
Abbott	X			X	X	X	X			X						X		X
Bailey	X	X	X	X	X	X	X					X				X		
Cooper		X	X									X				X		
Charles			X		X									X		X		
Dell	X	X	X			X	X							X		X		
Dimmock	X	X	X	X	X					X		X		X		X		
Ewart	X	X	X	X	X	X	X					X		X		X–	X	
Francis			X		X						X	X		X		X		
Gordon	X		X	X						X						X		
Harris	X	X	X	X			X							X	X			X
Ilson				X	X	X	X	X						X	X	X		
James	X		X		X		X			X				X				X
Kennedy	X	X	X			X	X	X	X		X		X		X			
Lowe	X						X	none necessary										X
Milward	X	X	X		X		X	X	X	X						X		
Norris	X		X			X				X		X		X		H	W–	N
Osborne				none				X							X	X		
Price						X		X	X					X	X	X		
Roberts	W			X		X		X	X							H	W	
Sanders	H				X	X			X					X	X	X		
Sheldon				none					X	(little)						X		
Stocks				none						X				X			X–	X
Tyson				none				none necessary								not applicable		
Underwood	X	X	X						X						X	X		
Vincent	X	X	X						X	(little)						X		
Williams			X			X		none necessary								X		
Yates			X	X					X						X	X		
	16	9	17	9	11	11	10	1	6	14	2	7	1	12	7	22	4	6

the people they visit are very weak: I was like that—very weak-minded. They've got to be strong. They should be able to take control of the situation. When I used to blow up at her, she would give me what-for back, but in a better manner. She got through to me.' ... 'He can be very straight and strong, and he'll make you listen, and say some harsh things; but I like him. He'll let you pour your heart out, and then he'll start and put you all back in place. I think you've got to be strict, but listen first.'

Mrs Bailey: 'Steve was great. He thought I was dodging him, and he left a note saying he wanted to see me. It was just that I was busy; but I *did* stay in and see him.'

Mr Cooper: 'He kept on at me [to pay the debts]. At one time I couldn't be bothered. I wasn't interested. I'd had that many let-downs. But he pushed me, and he really made me interested in other things.'

Mrs Ewart: 'If we go off on the wrong track, and we tell Steve, then he speaks to him [husband] and gets us right.'

Mrs Francis: 'She'll not let you rabbit away. She'll ask you questions—"How are you getting on?" and "Do you think this is upsetting you?" and that sort of thing. She sort of goes *into* it with you.'

Key:	In this table x implies a positive answer.
	w = wife only; h = husband only.
Kinds of firmness	(1) Instructing
	(2) Advising
	(3) Requiring certain standards of behaviour
	(4) Discouraging certain kinds of talk
	(5) Refusing inappropriate advice-giving
	(6) Refusing material aid
Setting limits	(7) Taking a man to work
	(8) Limiting clients' dependency, reducing the number of visits below the wishes of the clients
	(9) Steering discussion from or to particular subjects
	(10) Introducing discussion concerned to improve relationships with other agencies
	(11) Emphasizing the importance of paying debts, rent, etc.
	(12) Containing and discussing anger and distress
	(13) Avoiding or resolving collusions or manipulations
	(14) Helping clients to resolve phantasies
Clients' responses	a accepting the therapeutic value of limits
	r continuing to resent
	n taking no notice

Mrs Ilson: 'She's right understanding, and she's very forward [i.e. outspoken]. If you say something and she disagrees with you, she'll give you a straight answer. She won't hide it ... she doesn't agree with you all the time, and she doesn't believe you all the time. Some others [social workers] believe everything you say, but not Pam: many times we have a disagreement with each other—you know, like bringing the kids up, income, and one thing and another. She's straightforward, honest; we're just like two sisters.... She's very firm, and that's what I like about her.'

These comments indicate interdependence between an acceptable capacity to be firm (or the exercise of appropriate firmness) and the capacity for accurate empathy; this may be set out as a further hypothesis: that a client's acceptance of a social worker's directiveness depends (at least in part) upon his awareness of accurate empathy.

The next section will examine those attitudes in relationships (and perceptions of attitudes) which, in the views of the clients indicate the presence of empathy and promote awareness of it. We may conclude the present discussion, however, by reviewing the particular aspects of clients' behaviour towards which firmness was especially directed. Direct instruction and strongly worded advice were employed

> to get the house cleaned up,
> to prevent the abandoning of children,
> to prevent suicide,
> to get the rent or other debts paid,
> to look after children more conscientiously, and
> to get a man back to work.

Changes were demanded in standards of behaviour relating to

> cleanliness,
> school attendance, and
> violence in the marital relationship.

Discouraging certain kinds of talk was associated principally with

> protecting children from temper or from involvement in the intimacies of marital conflict

but was also used

> in marital rows, and
> to prevent the re-iteration of excuses for failure.

Refusing to give advice was associated exclusively with

marital disputes, and
parent-child quarrels

where manipulation of the worker's loyalties was attempted.

In this and preceding sections, I have described a blending of permissiveness and authority. The next section will be concerned with the attitudes, adopted and perceived, which contributed to clients' awareness of the presence of accurate empathy in social workers—to the feeling of being really understood. In addition to spontaneous and outgoing friendliness in the relationships, the way in which these other qualities are blended, which together form the common ground of all social work (whether described in terms of professional help or befriending), will depend on the social worker's accuracy in perception, his emotional integrity and self-discipline, and his views of his own obligation and purpose—his definition of his role. This definition implies, however, the existence of the reciprocal role of client. In no aspect of social work is the client's role more important and yet more uncertainly defined than in relation to the moral obligation and purpose of the social worker, and his use of authority. It is therefore of interest to note that clients in seven families, when speaking of the referral of other families to the Unit, made it clear that they expected certain standards of behaviour to be maintained by both clients and workers—that total permissiveness should not be expected from social workers, and that clients should accept obligations if they expect to be helped. This may be a further example of certain clients' identifying with the values of the social workers; if so, this identification was not related, so far as could be ascertained, to the outcome of work with the families concerned.

The Bailey, Cooper, Ewart, Kennedy and Sanders families all roundly condemned scroungers: 'We don't want to be cheeky [i.e. scrounge]. We don't want to push them.' 'We don't want them to feel that if we have a problem we can just pop along to the FSU. We don't want them to feel we're scroungers.' 'My brother has been in trouble, and has had help from the Unit, but [in a condemnatory tone] he never bothered to pay it back.' 'If I knew a family who was in trouble *through no fault of their own*, then I'd ask John [the Unit worker]—[but only] if they were *reliable*.' Mrs Price considered that the client has some responsibility for controlling the over-interference of the social worker. Mr Cooper and Mrs Stocks felt strongly that the Unit should not be bothered with petty problems. 'You shouldn't worry the Unit with trivial things, or things which you can sort out yourself.' But definitions can be difficult in this respect. 'I wouldn't like to bring him into family arguments—it would put too much on his shoulders. He's enough to do without ... trivialities.'

These observations are of special interest, coming from families whose lives have, in some cases, seemed morally chaotic to observers and referral agents in other services.

The clients' descriptions of the attitudes of their preferred social workers

Reference has been made to the relationship between acceptable directiveness and the social worker's capacity for accurate empathy. The assumption was made, in planning the research interviews, that the families' descriptions of their favourite workers would provide us with a guide to how an accurately empathetic relationship appears to a family.

The following comments made by some clients indicate the areas generally regarded as important. These will be followed by more precise information about the frequency with which individual factors were emphasized by clients and social workers.

First, importance was given to 'homeliness'. This word (or 'homely') was used by many families, and particularly emphasized by eleven. 'She'll just sit down and be comfortable.' (Dawson) 'I thought she was a smashing girl; when she used to come in, she'd say "Have you mashed yet? [i.e. made tea]".' (Lowe) 'I thought they'd be upperty ... they were right friendly, as though it were your relation instead of a social worker.' (Francis) 'It's easy [to get things off your chest] if they're not too snobbish.' (Price) 'They never let you feel as if you are poor; they never let you *think* that you're poor. They make you feel as if you are just talking to a neighbour or a friend.' (Bailey) 'They don't hold things against you ... they treat you as if you were ordinary. They're like a family to me; *closer* than a family.' (Charles)

This notion of homeliness is developed by some clients in two ways: first, to emphasize that the relationship does not feel like an official one, and second, that the workers took time and had patience. In our view, the workers' willingness to spend time was of particular importance; several clients spoke of their difficulties in finding the right words to describe their feelings and needs, and this was apparent sometimes when they were answering our questions. Thirteen clients made comments specially comparing official relationships (as impatient) and Unit relationships (as patient). For example:

> 'He'll have a laugh and a joke, he's interested in you ... he's not one who rushes in, collects his pound, and goes. He's interested in us as *people*, as a family.' (Cooper)

'They seem as if it's not too much trouble for them.' 'They've been very patient and understanding.' (Bailey)

'She'd sit down and take the trouble to find out what was the matter with you.' (Sanders)

'She helps you to talk, and listens to what you have to say ... she waits till you've had time to make up your own mind.' (Stocks)

'She was very patient. She was always trying to reach you—do you know what I mean?' (Price)

'She used to get it out of me and stop me worrying about things; we've talked about anything—even if it's only little things. It doesn't matter that it's only *little* things.' (Milward)

Officialdom seemed to have three characteristics in the replies of the families: keeping people waiting, interfering unasked, and being too free with advice. The Unit workers were therefore praised (by some twelve families) when they were prompt, avoided unacceptable interference, and allowed clients to reach decisions in their own time:

'When you go up there, you don't have to wait. Some places don't care how long you wait; but there they bring you a cup of coffee and ask how you are. When they come out after you've been kept waiting ... they say they are sorry.' (Bailey)

'They've always speeded things up.' (Dell)

'You only had to tell him, and by God he'd see to them. He had them [Supplementary Benefit] in tears one day.' (Ewart)

'They were in touch *straightaway*. I can always rely on them.' (Ilson)

But they do not interfere: one of the statutory services was described in this way, 'they make you feel frightened, they shout at you, they threaten you ... they make you feel as if you're a nobody—they make you feel like scuff ... [but] the Unit don't come unless you want them to come.' (Cooper) 'He wasn't one of those who looks round every five minutes, looking at what's happening.' (Sanders) 'If she was an official, we wouldn't talk about half the things we talk about.' (Francis)

On the delicate issue of giving advice: 'They don't give advice ... they say what they *think* you ought to do, but they don't say you've got to do it.... If they think you shouldn't have done something, they'll tell you "Well, I don't think you should have done it *that* way, wouldn't it be better *this* way?" but they don't dictate.' (Gordon)

'She wasn't the sort of person who ... tells you what to do—who stops you talking ... I don't think it's any good talking to a social worker who doesn't want your opinion.' (Stocks)

'They ask you in such a way that it's a pleasure to do it for them.' (Vincent)

Several clients emphasized the importance of trustworthiness and authority—the keeping of promises, the keeping of confidence, ('They go out of their way to keep their promises.' 'You can tell her things you wouldn't tell a neighbour,') the reliable authority of negotiations with other services, and preparedness to listen to all sides ('We can be arguing hell-for-leather, and she'll walk in and sit down, and say "Carry on, it's O.K., carry on"; she'll never get between us, unless we're really going mad, and then she'll step in.').

When families complained of any unsatisfactory experiences of the Unit's work, their comments related to the opposites of these qualities. Three clients recognized that husbands and wives have different ideas about what constitutes interference and suggested that this can create barriers within a marriage; in this situation, one suggested, the client will need to have less to do with the social worker than the social worker wants. Three clients felt that, in spite of the patience shown by their caseworkers, they were still too rushed in visits to find the words to say all they wanted to say. One family felt that, when they refer a family, they ought to be taken into the social worker's confidence with regard to his intentions.

Having isolated these qualities, however, one does not necessarily identify the essence of an empathetic relationship. As Mrs Francis commented: 'They've all been nice, but there was only the one I could *really* talk to ... when I've *really* felt comfortable. You could talk to *any* of them, but with Pam I could *really* tell my troubles.' A few clients tried to identify this special quality, and their successful attempts seemed to us to be worth recording here:

'He was better educated, he had more of a grasp; he *understood*
... I don't know how to classify it ... he knew the *basic*
things; he could see the difficulties we were up against. He could classify different sets of people.... He was educated, but homely with it.... [He could] somehow tell the genuine ones from the cheeky ones.' (Mr Sanders)

'They *can* understand us because they *want* to understand us.' (Mr Vincent)

'It's got to be on a friendly basis with me. It's no good them coming and just sitting and listening to you, and not caring a damn, you *know* they don't. They don't *feel* for you. But when you get friends—say, for instance, you get a black eye —they really *feel* it with you. I got that impression with Pat—if she saw me with a black eye, you felt as if *she* felt it as well.' (Mrs Underwood)

'She was hurt as well; she felt it as much as I felt it.' (Mrs Ilson)

Finally, families were asked to comment more generally (not only in relation to their favourite workers) about attributes desirable in the personalities of social workers. The social workers were asked similarly to guess what their families' answers had been to these questions. No check-list of personal qualities was employed and the replies consisted of spontaneous comments. There was close accord between the two sets of responses with, as we would expect, greater detail from the clients. In all, the families gave 112 comments and the social workers 90. These may be grouped together as in Table 17.

One hesitates to draw inferences from comments classified as loosely as those in the table, particularly as the groupings themselves are open to question: for example, 'spending enough time' might have been recorded as part of the 'understanding, caring and listening' group of factors. Broadly speaking, however, certain emphases in the responses are apparent. The importance to clients of friendliness was recognized, but with less emphasis, by the social workers. The workers, perhaps because of their professional orientation, gave particular weight to 'reliable emotional support', while clients gave similar weight to the importance of 'understanding and caring'. The relative importance placed by the families on moral goodness in social workers has been noted already, and is of interest here. It appears once again that the clients showed a greater concern for ethical qualities of relationship than we might have anticipated, especially considering the chronic reiteration of poverty in which many of the families lived.

A comment on worker-client relationships in terms of role-behaviour

Reference has been made to the problems and feelings of becoming a client: a process which adds new status and a new role to an existing set, and which may lead to the generation or increase of

TABLE 17 *The importance ascribed to attitudes in the relationships of social workers*

Factors	Number of clients' comments		Number of workers' comments	
Friendly	14		11	
spending enough time	6		1	
spontaneously wanting to help	10	43	12	27
equality in relationship	5			
not holding grudges	3		2	
a sense of humour	5		1	
Like a member of the family	9	9	4	4
Understanding, caring, listening	13		17	
nothing too much trouble	5	27	1	21
polite (not bossy)	9		3	
Reliable emotional support	7	16	15	26
Availability in crises	9		11	
Moral goodness; just	9	17	5	12
completely trustworthy	8		7	
		112		90

internal and external conflict. This problem was implicit in the families' comments about their expectations at referral; several clients drew attention to their fears of interference; the uncooperative husbands, discussed earlier, illustrate a further aspect of the problem; and comments have been made, and clients quoted, on the importance of sharing and obligation (variously described) as factors in the acceptability of social workers to families.

Clients varied, however, in the extent to which the client-role was resented. One possible explanation for this variation, suggested by the work of Elizabeth Bott (1957) and reflected in some comments made by Mr Vincent, is that this additional role is more easily accepted (that is to say, without strong positive or negative feelings) by clients who enjoy a supportive network of local family and friends.

Sometimes, however, a client's inability to accept the role of client may relate to the social worker's failure to recognize intrinsic conflicts within the existing role-set before he expects the client to assume this additional role. Mrs Gordon, for example, spoke with very considerable dislike of one agency because a social worker blamed her for leaving her children unattended at home while she pushed their dirty clothes in the pram to the nearest wash-house a mile away.

The firmness used by the social workers, and described earlier in this chapter, may be seen as the prescription of roles for clients whose role-competence was regarded as poor, either at certain times or in certain areas of performance. Mrs Gordon's dislike of the other agency is, in a way, the result of a role-prescription in which some simple facts were ignored and from which empathy was lacking.

In the light of the families' comments it appears that the acceptability or otherwise of role-prescribing in specific situations relates, at least in part, to the willingness of the social worker to accept, albeit temporarily, the roles with which the client endows him, however realistic or unrealistic these may be. Mr Ewart was physically violent from time to time towards his most recent social worker, whom he held in high esteem; on those occasions the worker had to be willing to be placed in and to accept the role of an enemy. Mrs Dell's manipulations were occasionally accepted (in respect of the relatively safe area of material aid), even though, because of their persistence, the social worker resisted the long-term role-prescription of being an all-giving person. It seems that roles were prescribed for each other (wittingly or unwittingly) by both clients and workers, and that the periods of equilibrium in casework were based on the tacit acceptance of these prescriptions by both. But in order to bring about changes in behaviour and feelings, or to off-set self-destructiveness or egocentricity in the client, the worker may consider it essential periodically to disrupt this equilibrium.

On those occasions when families complained in interview of the behaviour of social workers, or expressed dislike for them, the point at issue seemed to be, not these episodes of disequilibrium, but rather the worker's unchanging inflexibility of role, his refusal even temporarily to assume the role prescribed for him by the client. Mrs Ewart's condemnation of a caseworker as 'rotten' may partly have arisen not only because of the implied accusation of scrounging (for, as we have seen, she and her husband were among those who roundly condemned scrounging clients) but also because, by telling her never to return for financial help, he showed this kind of inflexibility in prescribing his own role and hers. He did not admit the possibility of an occasional return to the supplicant (or scrounger) and giver roles, but instead demanded consistency in one aspect of their future association. Her continuing condemnation of him exceeded, in emotional force, what might be expected as a response to a single denial of future help—a threat for which the Unit has subsequently made ample restitution.

Herbert Strean (1968), in writing of the problems of work with 'ego-fragmented' clients, has suggested that when a client lacks ego-consistency and behavioural integration, the caseworker needs to adopt an approach of considerable role-flexibility. In the same way as he might expect to respond to the role-uncertainties and inconsistencies of a young child, so with an adult in parallel difficulties he needs to be sometimes firm, sometimes friendly, sometimes very giving, sometimes refusing and limiting. When compared with the more usually defined attributes of a professional relationship, this responsiveness must appear unpredictable, even irresponsible. The only consistency to be found among divergent and discrepant behavioural responses may be their derivation from a single root of responsibility and concern. These attributes may not be readily detectable from an examination of the social worker's activities, one by one, but rather from the way in which the various qualities described in this chapter are blended in the spontaneous expression of his attitudes towards others. His responsive and responsible assumption of diverse roles may be the necessary reflection of his client's unpredictable yet not wholly random search for consistent and integrated patterns of behaviour.

Notes

Jackson (1973) presents similar findings from her study of the Islington FSU concerning the social workers' personal disclosures, the relationship of advising and befriending, and the use of authority—i.e. the social worker as both friend and official. She suggests that some intimate knowledge of the social worker is not only valued for itself by the client, but it increases his feeling that he is dealing with a real person, and it enables him to make use of the personal as well as the professional characteristics and strengths of the worker. Kadushin (1972, pp. 100-2) emphasizes the importance of warmth and spontaneity ('readiness') in the caseworker's relationships, and the value of his sharing his own life experiences when pertinent, in order to aid the client's identification with the worker. This seems to relate closely to the findings from the present study, but may be open to the objection, expressed by some of the social workers and set out fully in Chapter 8, that it sounds manipulative.

The relationships between clients' feelings of satisfaction and the emotional support and direct guidance of the social workers is studied in Mayer and Timms (1970, pp. 93-4). They suggest also that the combining of support, material aid and activity is compatible with clients' own views of problem-solving, and therefore facilitates the development of a close relationship within which psychologically sophisticated help may be made possible. However, this help was not, in their view, always compatible with the clients' knowing the social workers intimately. Thus, they conclude (and this is supported in the present study) that professional discretion is important in recognizing when intimacy and help would be incompatible for a particular client.

Blaine and McArthur (1958) found that even where therapists and patients disagreed on several significant parts of the therapeutic process, therapy was deemed by both to have been helpful where they agreed about the nature of the relationship, which the patients described as reassuring, reliable, and an experience of firm but accepting authority.

Gottschalk and Auerbach (1966) suggest that the client's perceptions of a therapist's behaviour should take into account the following dimensions: his understanding, accepting, independence-encouraging, authoritarianism, and his criticism/hostility. The implications of the present study are that the social workers and clients were alive to the importance of four of these dimensions, but perhaps less aware in their discussions with each other of the dimension of independence-encouraging. It is suggested that the ambiguity attaching to the idea of 'successful' work is partly associated with lack of emphasis on this dimension.

7
Changes in the families' lives

This chapter presents findings which cannot be other than tentative, and in respect of which caution must be exercised. The concern of the study has been with the subjective impressions of clients and social workers in regard to their relationships, needs, and the experience of working together. In this chapter also the outcome of work—or, rather, change in the families' social functioning (from whatever causes) during the period of contact—is considered through the eyes of the social worker rather than in relation to objective criteria. Gottschalk and Auerbach (1966) have observed that retrospective reports should be treated with caution: in the present study, we cannot be sure whether those received from the social workers were unduly optimistic or pessimistic. They have argued also that, in work of this kind, ultimate criteria of success still await definition: the present study will support their view when we consider the definitions of good and successful work variously expressed by the eleven social workers concerned in this study and by their Committee. In the following pages, therefore, where reference is made to perceived changes in social functioning, no criteria of success or failure are implied.

Plowman (1969) has suggested that, in considering the outcome of casework, reference should be made to three areas of the clients' functioning: various kinds of social adjustment; the relief of symptoms; and increases in self-insight. In the following analysis, the first six factors relate to Plowman's first area and the seventh and eighth factors to his second. No factors directly relevant to the third area were available in the context of this study, though some indications of this kind of outcome may lie in changes associated with the sixth, seventh and eighth factors.

In discussion with the social workers, they were invited to consider whether they had perceived any movement in the following eight areas of functioning:

(1) financial management;
(2) marital relationship (or relationship in a long-standing cohabitation);
(3) parent-child relationships;
(4) husband's attendance at work;
(5) children's social behaviour (in school, in clubs, in school attendance, in the commission of offences, etc.);
(6) the parents' individual competence in the roles of parent and spouse;
(7) the parents' ability to cope with inner distress (e.g. with the experience of depression, anxiety, anger);
(8) their coping with external pressures (e.g. sudden problems or demands, debt, court appearances).

It was not relevant to the situation of all families to look for change in each of these dimensions, either because their circumstances made certain dimensions inapplicable or because their functioning was perceived (by themselves and the social worker) as entirely adequate in certain respects at the time of referral. (In the latter case, however, any decline in competence is recorded.) No suggestion is intended that social work was responsible for any change (or lack of change).

The social workers were asked also to assess the effect on each family's competence of closing the case: whether competence in general would improve (or has improved) following closure; or was expected to remain at the same level; or would decline.

The views of the social workers on all these issues are set out in Table 18. Clients' feelings about the closing of cases are also recorded here: i.e. whether they are or would be glad about it; would have mixed feelings about it; or would be sorry. (Clients with surnames A to O are 'open'; from P to Y are 'closed'.)

It will be noted that, at the referral stage, seven families were thought to need help in all eight areas of functioning, nine in seven areas, four in six areas, three in five areas, three in four areas, and one in three areas. In the estimation of the social workers, two families had shown some improvement in all appropriate areas of functioning, eight in all save one area, and four in all save two. Thus, fourteen of the families (about half of the research group) showed some satisfactory movement. On the other hand, six families appeared to be experiencing greater difficulties than earlier in respect either of their financial management or of the husband's work attendance. The competence of the remaining seven families seemed little changed.

Following closure of the case, six families (three 'open' and

TABLE 18 *Perceived changes in social functioning (2)*

Family	Dimensions of functioning				Expectations of functioning after closure			Clients' feelings about closure		
	Improved	Same	Worse	Change not appropriate	Up	Same	Decline	Glad	Mixed	Sorry
Abbott	1, 2, 3, 8	4, 5, 6		7	X					X
Bailey	1, 7	2, 5, 6, 8		3, 4			X			X
Cooper	1, 6, 7, 8	2, 3, 5	4		X				X	
Charles	3, 6, 7	8		1, 2, 4, 5		X				X
Dell	1, 2, 5, 7, 8	3, 6	4				X			X
Dimmock	8	2, 3, 4, 6, 7	1	5		X			X	
Ewart	5	1, 2, 3, 4, 6, 7, 8					X			X
Francis	1, 2, 4, 6, 7, 8			3, 5		X				X
Gordon	1, 2, 3, 6, 7, 8	4		5	X				X	
Harris	1, 2, 5, 6	3, 7, 8		4			X			X
Ilson	2, 3, 5, 6, 7, 8	4		1		X				X
James	3, 6, 7	2, 5	4	1, 8		X			X	
Kennedy	1, 2, 5, 7, 8	3, 4		5			X		X	
Lowe	2, 6, 7, 8	5		1, 3, 4			X		X	
Milward	2, 5, 6, 7	1, 3, 4, 8					X			X
Norris	3, 4, 5	2, 6, 7, 8	1				X		X	
Osborne	3, 6, 7, 8	4		1, 2, 5		X		X		
Price	2, 7*	6		1, 3, 4, 5, 8			X			X
Roberts	2, 3, 5*	1, 6, 7, 8		4	X				X	
Sanders	2, 3, 7†	6, 8		1, 4, 5		X		X	X	
Sheldon	1, 2, 6, 7, 8	3		4, 5			X		X	
Stocks	6, 7, 8	1, 2, 3, 4		5			X			X
Tyson	3, 7	6, 8		1, 2, 4, 5		X			X	
Underwood	1, 2, 3, 5, 6, 7, 8†			4	X		X			
Vincent	1, 2, 3, 5, 8†	6, 7	4			X			X	•
Williams	1, 2, 4, 5, 6, 7	3, 8			X				X	
Yates	3, 7, 8	5		1, 2, 4, 6		X				X

* work more successful with husband
† work more successful with wife; no work undertaken with Mr Underwood

TABLE 19 *Frequency of change in the factors of social functioning*

Factor no.	All cases				Open cases				Closed cases			
	I	U	W	N/A	I	U	W	N/A	I	U	W	N/A
1	12	4	2	9	8	2	2	5	4	2		4
2	16	7		4	9	6		2	7	1		2
3	13	10		4	7	7		3	6	3		1
4	3	9	4	11	2	8	3	4	1	1	1	7
5	10	6		11	6	5		6	4	1		5
6	15	11		1	11	6			4	5		1
7	20	6		1	12	4		1	8	2		
8	15	10		2	10	6		1	5	4		1

I=Improved; U=Unchanged; W=Worse; N/A=Change not appropriate

three 'closed') were assessed as likely to achieve further competence. On the other hand, the competence of eleven families would be likely to decline following closure. This latter expectation is not apparently related to the extent of achievement within the period of contact, nor to the feelings of the clients about closure. But in this respect, it may be significant that only three families said that they would be glad to end their contact with the Unit.

Table 19 indicates the frequency with which each of the eight areas of functioning appears in the categories Improved, Unchanged, Worse, or Change not Appropriate. It appears from this that the areas of functioning which, in the social workers' view, needed least attention initially were the husband's work attendance, the behaviour of the children, and the family's general financial management. (The findings for the first and third of these factors are particularly surprising, in view of the nature of the families' problems at intake.) If we consider aspects of social functioning rather than the forms in which problems were presented, it seems that the clients' greatest difficulties *as perceived by their social workers* lay in intra-familial role-performances and in the parents' incapacities to cope with inner distresses (mainly of depression and anxiety), and with feelings of panic or despair in the face of external pressures.

It is possible that these findings reflect in part the professional ideologies of the workers, or their assessment of the nature of their expertise. On the other hand, we have seen that the families interviewed were, for the most part at least, satisfied with the help they received; furthermore, a high level of congruence was discovered between the problems presented and the help offered. If we accept the social workers' assessments, then the conclusion seems to be that the Unit's clients need particular help in their intra-familial role-performances, and in respect of their personal feelings of distress; and that the Unit's greatest success lies in the help provided in those areas. It is relevant to recall at this point the importance accorded to the feelings and health of wives as topics of discussion during the social workers' visits. It seems likely, moreover, that the concerned and warm relationships described in the last chapter would be particularly effective as antidotes to feelings of ineptitude, depression, anxiety and panic, and might indirectly have some positive effect on marital relationships. At the other extreme, in only three families was positive change recorded in the work-performance of the husbands, while that of four others had declined.

These findings have a bearing on the final section of this study, in which an attempt will be made to examine the meanings ascribed to the notions 'good' and 'successful' social work. In spite of the emphasis on material needs and provisions in the Unit's work, it seems likely that the greatest single impact upon the clients' perceptions of the services received was made by the quality of relationships formed with the social workers; and that functional changes were most apparent in the area of personal and family feelings. In complement to this, the suggestion has been made that emphasis upon the intimacy of relationships may militate against the development in the client of a sense of long-term purpose; and that, similarly, the Unit's work was least effective (in the opinions of the social workers) in those areas of a client's life which are related to his performance outside the family, and in which he is judged as socially successful or unsuccessful without regard to his personal feelings.

We would expect, therefore, in the work of the Unit, that definitions of 'successful' work are likely to be equivocal and ambiguous.

A note on the findings for sub-groupings

In Chapter 2, mention was made of sub-groupings of families among the twenty-seven. Relevant findings of the study are now considered in relation to these sub-groupings.

Unsupported mothers There were five in all at referral (Mrs Charles, Mrs Lowe, Mrs Osborne, Mrs Tyson and Mrs Yates). Mrs Lowe subsequently cohabited, and Mrs Harris was widowed. The initial assumption was that women in this situation would develop a more intense relationship with their caseworker, or would identify more closely with the caseworker, than would women living with their husbands.

All six women, except Mrs Osborne who felt too confused to answer this question, overestimated their length of contact with the Unit by between one and three years. We have suggested earlier that overestimates may indicate closeness in relationship. At the same time, only three women in this group were thought to have 'affectionate' relationships with their most recent caseworkers, and three expressed no particular preference for one caseworker more than another. It may be, therefore, that any closeness in relationship was expressed more as reliance on the agency, or as identifying with the values and objectives of the caseworkers, than by particular feelings of affection. Four relevant findings are these:

(1) the four women who were unsupported mothers throughout their contact with the Unit (i.e. excluding Mrs Harris and Mrs Lowe) all regarded 'emotional support' as the most helpful form of help; it should be remembered, however, that this related closely to their own referral needs;
(2) the caseworkers indicated that it was much less necessary to use firmness and to set limits in their work with these women than, with other parents;
(3) in regard to the changes in their social functioning, the caseworkers indicated a better than average improvement for Mrs Charles, Mrs Osborne, and Mrs Yates, but not for Mrs Tyson; but
(4) all four were expected to be able to maintain their competence following the closing of the case.

A possible conclusion, therefore, is that unsupported mothers do not enter into closer personal relationships with individual caseworkers than other groups, but are more likely to identify with their values and standards.

Families who have worked with only one worker These families were Dimmock, Tyson, Underwood and Yates. Here again the initial assumption was made that contact with only one worker would lead to an emotionally more intense relationship than occurs in situations where there have been changes of worker; and that a greater identification might be found with the values and objectives of the caseworker.

The evidence from these families does not support either view. Though three specified 'emotional support' as the most helpful form of help, this related to their referral needs rather than to their experience of being helped. No family seemed to express 'affectionate' feelings for the caseworker, though three considerably overestimated the period of contact, and were thought to have close though not affectionate relationships. There was no significant difference between these and other families in the worker's exercise of firmness and the setting of limits; nor in the changes in social functioning.

No special advantage, therefore, seems to have accrued from avoiding changes of worker.

Families whose period of contact with the Unit was considerably longer than that of the main group (Harris, Milward, Norris and Sanders) The findings suggest no important difference between this and the main group in respect of their opinions about the most helpful forms of help, their estimate of the length of contact, or the quality of their relationships with particular workers. Three of these families are within the open cases category; all of them are below the average in respect of changes in social functioning and of the expectations of caseworkers concerning their capacity to manage without help.

In brief, these seem to be long-term cases quite simply because movement is slower and their problems were intractable. They do not appear to form closer relationships with their caseworkers, in spite of the length of contact.

The responses of families in the 'open' and 'closed' categories It was expected that, after closure, memories of the casework process would moderate in such a way as to make the relationship between caseworker and family seem less intense than it may in fact have been during the process of help. This seems to have occurred: less overt affection was expressed among the 'closed' families, and the workers also recalled the clients' attitudes towards them in less affectionate terms. The workers seemed to consider that families had felt less confidence in them than their current families, but this was not supported by the recorded comments of the families: in terms of confidence in the workers, no difference was found between the two groups.

As observed earlier, the workers recall exercising less firmness with this group. This may be a reflection of recent changes in the approach of caseworkers; or it may be a further indication that both sides remember the relationship with less emotional intensity, whether affectionate or firm, once the case is closed. Reduction in intensity of feeling does not, however, indicate any reduction in clients' appreciation of the 'emotional' kinds of help received. When asked for their memories of the most helpful form of help, 'closed' families placed less emphasis on material and financial matters than did 'open' families.

Memories of fact rather than of feeling are also not significantly reduced following closure. There was no difference between the two groups in the proportion of families who could accurately recall the length of their contact with the Unit. (None of the 'closed' families underestimated this period, and proportionally more overestimated it, but the significance is doubtful.) Moreover, the clarity of memory of their referral situations and needs was only slightly less vivid among the 'closed' families.

With regard to changes in social functioning during the period of casework, the caseworkers' estimates for the two groups were compared with regard to those factors which needed help at referral. It appears that, in spite of the lessening in intensity of feeling (positive feeling particularly) in the memories of both workers and clients when they recall their relationships, 'closed' families have improved more than 'open' families in their overall social competence. 'Closed' cases appear more frequently in the 'improved' category, 'open' cases more frequently in the 'unchanged' category; the frequency of 'worse' is the same.

To sum up: when families end their contact with social workers, it seems that their memory of facts does not decline significantly, but that the intensity of relationship is less vividly recalled. Among social workers, memories of both facts of a case and the feelings within it grow less vivid.

Notes

Most studies of the outcome of casework and psychotherapy emphasize the need for caution in retrospective evaluations. For example, Powers and Witner (1951) show a lack of correspondence between the measured outcome of social work in a programme of delinquency prevention and the positive evaluation accorded to the programme by the social workers and clients involved. Parad (1965), similarly, advocates that the study of outcome in crisis intervention can be undertaken effectively only within the clients' experience of current crisis. Caution in this matter readily turns into pessimism when one reviews the studies of effectiveness by, e.g., Powers and Witner (1951), Eysenck (1952) and Meyer (1965): 'we must conclude that, with respect to all of the measures we have used to examine the effects of the treatment program, only a minimal effect can be found' (Meyer, p. 204). Brown (1968) and Mullen (1972) demonstrate small but not statistically significant improvements in functioning within family life. In relation to the present study, however, it is of interest that the area of change noted by Brown and Mullen lay *within* family life rather than in

CHANGES IN THE FAMILIES' LIVES

individual members' external relationships. Studies relevant to changes in the seventh and eighth factors listed in this chapter are Assum and Levy (1948), Cofer and Chance (1950) and Grummon and John, in Rogers and Dymond (1954).

8
'Good' and 'successful' work

The place of ethical factors

In the family interviews, clients were asked to justify their preferences for particular social workers: most were able to do so without difficulty, and thus we have been able to isolate some aspects of personality which, in terms of the frequency with which they were mentioned, were evidently important in making the help of the agency acceptable to the families. Refinement of these ideas was made possible by two further questions, concerning what the clients had disliked in their contacts with social workers in general, and about the changes they thought had taken place in their relationships with other social services. These questions were followed by the more general enquiry, 'What do you think makes a helpful social worker?' Most clients offered additional information at this point, and this was the most frequent continuing topic of conversation after the formal close of the research interview.

These findings have been set out in Chapter 6. It has been suggested there that the clients gave considerable weight to relationship factors and ethical considerations in some form. Speed and efficiency in the provision of service was less frequently mentioned, and was sometimes subsumed in the clients' regard for their caseworkers' dependability and availability in crises. As it happened, the social workers in this study, judged by the case-records as well as by the comments of the families, were all prompt in offering various kinds of service; and thus no test could be made how far the apparent primacy of place given by the clients to relationship and ethical considerations would have been maintained if a personally acceptable caseworker were also a slow or incompetent provider of services. It could be argued, of course, that the ethical integrity of a social worker would ensure that he acted promptly on his clients' behalf; but, as suggested elsewhere, the administrative flexibility and responsiveness of an agency may be important influences on the client's perception of the performance of the individual social worker, and on the client's judgment not only of the social worker's efficiency but also of his personal concern and sincerity. It would be interesting, therefore, to test how far the reasons given by the families in this study for preferring particular social workers would be maintained if they were receiving visits from workers from agencies whose administrative responsiveness to their needs was less prompt. (Although Mr and Mrs Williams had high regard for a caseworker who had not been their most efficient helper, there is little doubt from the records that he was efficient enough.)

While the emphasis placed by the families on the ethical and emotional goodness of their caseworkers is impressive, it does not in itself permit comparisons of the *relative* importance of humane factors and perceived efficiency within clients' views of effective social work practice.

Befriending and social functioning

In Chapter 7, an examination was made of the social workers' opinions of changes in the social functioning of families during the period of contact. This suggested that the Unit's kind of approach may have been more influential in relation to changes in the performance of intra-familial roles and in the self-related feelings of clients (e.g. allaying panic and anxiety, increasing self-esteem) than in extra-familial roles, irrespective of the nature of the problems presented at the start of contact between family and Unit. It has been suggested also that the quality of relationships established by the social workers may have led the families to value these relationships as separate from and not readily related to long-term problem-solving or to long-term changes in role-behaviour. Put in another way: close relationships of the kind described in this study are effective in helping people to feel differently about themselves; this may have a spin-off effect in the ways in which they relate to each other in marriage, and in which they cope with feelings of crisis; but in so far as relationships are perceived by clients as truly friendly, they are unlikely to be perceived also as related to long-term purpose. Friendships are supports in short-term needs, but are not regarded as having a long-term purpose.

Ambiguity may therefore enter the notion of successful social work by way of the strength of relationship upon which it is based. The end-products of social work (whether for a caseworker, neighbourhood worker, welfare rights activist, or houseparent) may become increasingly difficult to state, the more he emphasizes the quality of the process by which they are to be achieved.

The relationship between 'good' and 'successful'
The next stage of the study therefore required an exploration of the ideas of good and successful work held by the social workers themselves, in the expectation that the ambiguity of this situation would be present in their replies, precisely because of the close and empathetic relationships they had established with many of their clients. How far is personal concern for somebody compatible with the intention of changing him? How far is change in another person to be welcomed as a by-product of one's relationship with him, rather than as the *raison d'être*, and only justification, for forming the relationship?

Questions of this kind no doubt lie at the root of much of the disquiet and uncertainty expressed by social workers and students about practice (or, at least, some practices) in formal and bureaucratized social services. On the one hand, social workers are increasingly challenged to demonstrate that their activities 'work'. This challenge, if presented within or directed towards a formal service—particularly a statutory one—seems to presuppose that the criteria of effectiveness are related either to the kinds of change deemed to be administratively desirable, or to the assumed validity of some political or psychiatric recipes for the 'good life'—or, at least, for the historically inevitable one. If the criteria are administrative, then the only permitted evidence consists of changes measured by externally perceived behavioural adaptations, and sufficiently rapid to be accountable within the confines and limitations of an annual report: for example, how many men 'were got back into' employment, without regard for the circumstances of their unemployment. If the criteria are political or psychiatric, then the evidence must be pared down to a theoretical orientation which may wholly set aside the professional primacy, in all social work, of the 'felt needs' of individuals and the embarrassments of what individual clients actually say about their likes, wants, fears, hopes and aspirations.

On the other hand, as suggested by the growing numbers of voluntary and 'alternative' (and 'underground') opportunities for social intervention, the fashion for 'grass-roots' thinking and action, and the commitment to 'detached' work, there is an increasing body of opinion that to make friendly relationships with people is justifiable in itself—it is its own good, and justifiable only in its own terms—and that to speak of a reason for forming a relationship is potentially unethical.

The eleven social workers were asked (informally and at length) for their opinion about 'what makes a good and successful caseworker'. Their replies may be summarized as follows.

Seven distinguished between the ideas 'good' and 'successful' when applied to social work practice. The basis of the distinction was that 'success' relates to the achievements and movements made by the client; thus a successful caseworker is one who causes the client to change. 'Good' relates to the worker's input of feelings and beliefs, and does not necessarily imply change in the client. The other four workers considered that good and successful work cannot be separated in this way, not because the notions are identical but because, in social work, success is to be regarded as depending on, and possibly rooted in, the goodness of the social worker; i.e. that one cannot be a successful caseworker unless one has certain ethically desirable attributes, or is concerned to develop and express such attributes in situations where they are not spontaneously experienced. In both groups of caseworkers, the same ethical factors were mentioned, and two of those who distinguished between good and successful work suggested that goodness is a prerequisite of success. For example, 'a client's success may depend on the worker being a good person, or a good parent-figure'; 'good refers to certain identifiable qualities of relationship which are essential to all successful work, whereas the idea of success is a variable notion wholly dependent on the circumstances of the case'; 'it is important not to detach "good" from "successful", for success in casework refers to the use made of the good'. (This last respondent suggested that although 'success' relates to the achievement of change in, by and with the client, the 'good' used refers to the emotional and ethical input of both worker and client.)

Factors suggested as components in the idea of good casework may be listed as follows: numbers in brackets refer to the frequencies with which factors were mentioned:

(1) (a) accountability of the worker jointly to his client, his agency and his profession (shown by persistence and reliability in caring for clients, remaining conscientious in humdrum work situations, and preserving ethical awareness) (3);
 (b) ethical and moral integrity (4);
 (c) patience and acceptance of clients' feelings without assuming total moral relativity (4);
(2) (a) sensitivity to a client's own perceptions of himself, his situation and his caseworker; achieving sensitivity even though the relationship is not a close one (6);
 (b) realistic awareness of the complexity of a client's experiences (3);

(c) unforced understanding and respect   (3);
(3) caring without making emotional demands or adding personal emotional burdens to the client   (2);
(4) (a) helping people to become self-reliant; providing a safe context for personal growth   (3);
(b) making constructive use of a relationship to achieve social ends agreed with the client   (6).

It appears that 'good casework' in the views of these respondents formed the basis of achievement but was not in itself identified with achievement. It safeguarded the feelings, needs and rights of clients in the processes of change.

Factors suggested in the idea of successful casework were:

(1) the client achieves greater insight   (3);
(2) the client achieves agreed goals in his personal relationships or role performance; he is more competent in meeting the demands of his own life   (7);
(3) (a) expeditious management by the worker of presented problems and/or immediate crises   (5);
(b) achieving changes that lead to the closing of the case   (2);
(c) a variable concept rooted in the relationships of aspects of the worker's and client's social responsibilities and actions   (1);
(4) a moral or administrative imperative experienced by the caseworker   (1).

It will be evident that, for some workers, the use of the word 'success' carried anxieties concerning the achievement of short-term expedients without regard to longer-term feelings and needs; the fear that speed and efficiency in effecting change may be detrimental to the client. Success was often seen, broadly speaking, either in terms of the client's worthwhile achievements or of the worker's more suspect activities; pressure on the worker, matched by pressure on the client. Two workers who saw success in terms of the worker's (rather than the client's) achievement considered the concept of success to be of dubious value because it may lead, consciously or unconsciously, to the oversimplification of problems by workers in order to obtain a sense of achievement through the implementing of spurious solutions. The word 'success', it was thought, encourages workers to ignore the presence of constellations of problems in favour of the single aspect which can most readily (even unscrupulously) be manipulated; whereas the problems with which caseworkers deal were described in terms of stresses dispersed over several interlocking systems of experience and feeling. Another caseworker spoke of the need sometimes to avoid seeking the pleasure of success achieved by making people (clients or administrators) happy in the short-term; long-term achievement may sometimes be possible only through the continuation of short-term unhappiness.

To sum up the replies of the caseworkers: 'successful casework' should properly be related to the recognition of long-term goals shared with clients, to the use of the available 'good', to the worker's awareness of his limitations and capacities, to a shared regard for the interactions of long-term and short-term achievements, and to an awareness of professional purpose. But 'success' is often detached from these considerations and thus dangerously simplified to serve ends other than the well-being of the client.

The Committee interview

The Sheffield FSU Committee was later interviewed within an ordinary business meeting. Twelve members were present. The intention was to discover how far the complexity of this issue was experienced in the same terms by a group further removed from the immediate day-to-day pressures of casework practice, and who might be expected (for the purposes of fund-raising, not least) to have an administrative regard for demonstrable success. The interview took the form of a discussion among members of the following questions:

(1) What factors would the Committee consider in judging work to be successful?
(2) Is a distinction possible and desirable between good and successful work? (If so, how are they related?) (Are goals conceived as long-term or short-term, and who sets them?)
(3) To whom is the caseworker accountable?

The answers were provided by contributions from all members (except two Unit caseworkers who were asked to remain silent and unexpressive). The Unit Organizer was absent because of illness. Although different members produced different ideas—all of which are summarized below—no incompatibility was found between them.

(1) Criteria of success
(a) Long-term considerations were mentioned first: the Unit's purpose can be judged only with regard to the lives achieved by the children of the present families.
(b) 'Short-term work may appear to be successful, but we

cannot know it is except by the children making a better life for themselves in the future.'
  (c) In the short-term, success criteria were listed as:
    (i) the achievement by clients of self-esteem. 'First they develop confidence in the workers; then they gain confidence in dealing with other people';
    (ii) children attending school more regularly;
    (iii) fathers no longer returning to prison, no longer unemployed, and—more important in the Committee's view—becoming increasingly involved in the lives of their own families;
    (iv) improved morale and health of the wife and mother.
(2) Good and successful work
  Discussion established agreement in the following matters (in order):
  (a) 'good' and 'successful' are inseparable ideas in the practice of casework; but
  (b) 'good' implies values, whereas 'success' is variable according to the individual case;
  (c) a good caseworker is one who maintains his own morale, is able to overcome his own tendencies to depression and anxiety; he can tolerate lack of short-term success;
  (d) success in casework arises (i) out of the worker's goodness, as defined earlier, and (ii) out of arriving at an agreement with the client concerning the goals to be achieved;
  (e) in addition, a caseworker who is both good and successful is one who does not close cases following apparent but shortlived success, and whose personality is 'well-integrated'.
(3) The accountability of the worker
  The Committee considered that the worker is accountable to the family, the agency, the profession and the community. Accountability to the family was given, marginally, first place; the general view was that the worker should seek in each case to balance all four areas of responsibility without seeking an order of ranking applicable to all situations. When conflict arises between these responsibilities, the Committee considered the answer should be sought in the ethical convictions of the individual worker.

It appears that the Committee's views concerning success criteria, and their ideas of good work and of accountability, are largely in accord with the views of their caseworkers. Throughout the study it seemed likely that the relaxed and generous way in which the caseworkers allowed us to share their work, their families and their ideas, indicated the presence of administrative and policy backing with which they felt at ease.

Disagreement and disaffection would have produced a more exciting chapter, but the agreement present in this situation may serve as a model for the consideration of three groups of ideas and hypotheses related to success and purpose in social work. First, the responsiveness of workers to clients, *and their acceptability to clients*, cannot be divorced from the workers' own experiences of support and agreement from administrators and policy-makers. Second, success in social work cannot be considered in isolation from ethical and relationship issues. To divorce definitions of success from ethical considerations would leave the social workers at risk of condemnation as cynical manipulators, and in a professional limbo; to divorce measures of success from considerations of personal relationships would be to deny the validity of experiences upon which the clients themselves placed considerable weight, and which appear, to some clients at least, as inseparable from their experience of, and respect for, ethical values. Third, to talk of successful casework requires the consideration of long-term and short-term goals and achievements, and also of the causal and experiential connections between the two.

Notes

Eysenck (1952) concluded that 'there appears to be an inverse correlation between recovery and psychotherapy: the more psychotherapy, the smaller the recovery rate'. The present study is not concerned with objectively measured outcome, but Eysenck's conclusion may be not without some relevance to discussion of the increasing ambiguity within the notion of 'success' as client-worker relationships become friendly and intimate. Truax and Carkhuff (1967) concluded that the average effects of therapeutic intervention are about the same as for normal living; but they considered that there is some evidence of successful outcome among certain exceptional therapists. The present study was not concerned with exceptional therapists—some or all of the social workers may have been exceptional people, but making this identification was not the purpose of the study. The social workers may well, however, have been employed in exceptional work conditions—in relation, for example, to caseloads, personal freedoms and administrative support. An important area of further study in social work would be to identify the influence of work conditions on the perceived effectiveness of social workers, both in their own opinions and in the opinions of their clients.

Reference has been made, without definition, to 'accurate empathy'. The meaning of this phrase is well-expressed by Truax (1967): 'accurate empathy involves both the sensitivity to current feelings and the verbal facility to communicate this understanding in a language attuned to the client's current feelings.... At a high level of accurate empathy, the message "I am with you" is unmistakably clear ...: the therapist's remarks fit in just right with the client's mood and intent'. It has been shown earlier how, in the clients' opinions of two students, a lack of skill in relationships was perceived as a lack of concern, irrespective of the students' inner feelings of concern (even commitment) to helping these clients. This situation might be indicative of inaccurate empathy. Reid and Epstein (1972) have commented, 'The practitioner's internal state becomes important only as it is communicated to the client, and even then its importance is secondary to what is, in fact, communicated.'

Similarly, Mayer and Timms (1970, pp. 145, 147) discuss the question whether social workers sufficiently familiarize their clients with what they are trying to do, especially with working-class clients who do not readily think in interactional terms. 'Unless clients understand what their workers are about, an approach of this type (insight-oriented therapy) is bound to fail.' As we have seen, the social workers in the present study rooted their more 'professional' helping techniques in an ongoing friendliness with their families, through which, we may suppose, the clients gradually came to know what they were about. As Meltzoff and Kornreich (1970) have suggested (p. 172), 'success' involves the values, goals and aspirations of the perceivers (both client and worker).

9
Summary, conclusions and suggestions

There were three purposes in this study: first, to discover similarities and differences in the recollections of clients and caseworkers concerning the component parts of the casework process, and in particular to consider and compare those components which clients considered to be good in some way, so that some indicators of success would be suggested. Second, to extend our understanding of clients' impressions of casework by interviewing some 'multi-problem' families; and to discover whether families whose intelligence is often thought to be less and whose circumstances more universally disturbed than those of other clients could make a sustained contribution to discussions of the qualities and values of social work relationships. Third, to formulate hypotheses, for testing in other studies, concerning casework processes in general and factors associated with definitions of successful and purposeful practice.

'Clients are those citizens who experience what social services call help and who live with the results of that help' (Pinker 1971). Their experiences have been my main concern, and I was impressed by and grateful for the clarity with which they described them. Setting aside the manner in which the families have individually conducted their affairs, the moral and ethical standards they admired were frequently identical with those which the social workers were concerned to promote. Nearly half the families made thoughtful and socially acceptable attempts to meet their problems unaided before referral. When things went wrong for them, and when in some cases their responses have been externally judged as reckless and irresponsible, it seems that wilfulness was less a factor than incapacity. Like the rest of us—though sometimes with more dramatic results—they have done the things they did not want to do, and have not done the things they meant to do.

SUMMARY, CONCLUSIONS AND SUGGESTIONS

The families were some of those caught up in what is currently called 'the cycle of deprivation'. (Five families were second-generation FSU families.) The national study showed that the twenty-seven families interviewed were representative of those known to FSUs nationally: in relation to other families in the community, they were noticeable for the number and lesser intelligence (and other special needs) of children, the high unemployment rate of fathers, the prevalence of serious debts, and their frequent and repeated contacts with criminal and domestic courts.

In this study, the families and their most recent caseworkers were interviewed as to their recollections of

- the process of referral, and initial situations and expectations;
- the families' problems at referral and the degree of relevance in the help initially offered;
- the scope of helping, the subjects discussed and avoided, and the mode of help deemed to be of greatest significance;
- the length of contact and the nature of clients' preference for particular workers;
- the quality of worker-family relationships, with special regard to the intimacy, authority and acceptable attitudes contained in those relationships;
- and notions of good and successful work.

The findings are summarized below, followed by a note of the consequential hypotheses which may be derived from these findings, and finally by a statement of opinions relating to ideas of success and purpose in social work practice as a whole.

A summary of findings

1 Feelings and circumstances at referral Referral was inadequately performed in at least twelve of the twenty-seven cases, where families were wholly unaware of the Unit's functions, helping capacities, and attitudes in work. Seventeen families did not realize that the Unit's service was not part of the local authority's provision.

In the absence of more adequate preparation, clients' expectations of the Unit related either to experience (positively or negatively distorted) of other services, or to clients' hopes and fears projected on to the Unit. Expectations were further confused by the ambiguity of clients' relationships with other social services in all but six cases.

The vivid and accurate memories of referral suggested the intensity of feelings present at that time.

Before their referral, twelve families had made thoughtful and

SUMMARY, CONCLUSIONS AND SUGGESTIONS

socially acceptable attempts to solve their own problems; eight were emotionally adrift at that time; in only five cases did the families seek to deal with their problems by unacceptable and unsatisfactory means.

2 *Needs and help at referral* Twenty-three families mentioned material needs and debts as their major referral problems, but this did not indicate the mode of help or content of discussion to which they all gave primary value.

Twenty-five families were satisfied with the help they initially received because it related to their problems as they presented them (not necessarily in quantity, but in kind). A high degree of congruence was found between the needs presented and the initial modes of helping.

Some clients seemed to include or to imply emotional difficulties by their presentation of material needs; this certainly was the case with five families, two of whom indirectly acknowledged this in their choice of non-material help as the most valuable to them. It has been suggested, in respect of clients' memories of the main area of their discussions with caseworkers, that although material aid retains primacy in their recollections, it was not necessarily the family's only (or even major) objective in seeking help.

3 *Helping* Here, as elsewhere, clients' memories were never found to be false, and there were no discrepancies between them and the recollections of the caseworkers. Clients and workers sometimes omitted or forgot detail, however, and the evidence of the records was therefore of importance.

Material help was made available to twenty-six families in some form. Clients more readily remembered (or spoke of) help with clothes than with furniture or loans. It has been suggested that this selectivity may be based on (a) varying sensitivity, (b) the relative quality of the clothing and the furniture provided (both objectively and possibly symbolically), and (c) the closer temporal relationship between the provision of clothing and major feelings of anxiety and crisis.

Families did not usually regard the Unit House as the 'proper' place for interviews. Home visits were the norm, and took place (on average) weekly throughout the period of contact.

An attempt was made to draw a distinction between 'professional casework help' and 'befriending', largely in terms of the need for self-discipline in the worker and of his intentions to bring about changes in clients' attitudes and capacities. But the distinction was far from clear in practice, partly because it was not perceived in the same terms by clients as by caseworkers. What a caseworker might judge as lack of skill may be perceived and experienced by the client as a lack of friendly concern. On the other hand, some clients were aware of the need for professional detachment in some form and on some occasions.

In this study, the caseworkers regarded befriending as the norm: i.e. they emphasized support rather than insight-giving help. It is likely that this norm was the outcome of (a) the persistence of relationships over a long period; (b) the linking between material and emotional problems (noted above), and the resulting implications of style when work involves continuing help in at least two modes at the same time; and (c) the lack felt by several families of adequate support from relatives, neighbours and friends—a lack which workers sometimes filled spontaneously in addition to carrying out their professional tasks or assuming more professional roles. In six cases, befriending was the workers' preferred mode of help—where it was thought that any movement towards 'insight' would be inappropriate or destructive. In general, it appeared that for both workers and clients—so far as could be assessed—professional modes of help and befriending were not mutually exclusive activities in the work with a family over a long period of time.

In all but a few cases, the range of help and service extended well beyond the requests at referral.

It has been suggested that, in work with husbands/fathers who needed to appear physically and morally dominant at home, interviews at home or at the agency were not appropriate.

4 *Areas of discussion* The overall ranking of areas of discussion in terms of their frequency was:

(1) money and material problems;
(2) wife's health and feelings;
(3) care of children;
(4) marital relationships (mainly introduced by the worker).

(Matters relating to the husband were rarely recalled by clients or workers as significant.) But eleven families, and the caseworkers for three others, considered that discussions of the wife's health and feelings had been the most important topic; money and material needs were given primary importance in only seven families.

The major area of avoidance by clients was in relation to marital relationships; this was a difficulty, however, in only six families. Only three families appear persistently to have avoided discussion of their personal responsibilities generally (i.e. only three could with some justification be regarded as 'irresponsible' families). Dishonesty was a significant factor, however, in discussions with seven families. In a further six, important information had sometimes been withheld from the caseworker.

SUMMARY, CONCLUSIONS AND SUGGESTIONS

On the whole, clients selected as the most valuable kind of help the one most closely related to their own referral needs. In recalling this help, workers' and clients' views coincided in seventeen cases; in seven others, workers mistakenly assumed congruence.

In general, irrespective of the intimacy of current relationships between workers and clients, the memories and recollections of events tended to diverge. We found that clients' recollections were generally more vivid and a little more dependable.

5 *Relationships* It was hoped initially to be able to test whether clients' satisfactions were related to the extent of their identification with the workers' value-systems but, as virtually all clients were satisfied by the help received, these two factors could not be tested against each other. A very tentative link is suggested between clients' identifications with workers' values and the extent of change in their social functioning.

With regard to the length of contact between clients and workers, clients tended to overestimate, and workers to underestimate.

Warm relationships existed generally between workers and clients. A few families expressed no preference for any one worker in particular, and it seemed reasonable to regard them as families whose relationship was with the agency rather than with a worker. Where clients stated preferences for particular workers, these were accurately assessed by the current or most recent workers in thirteen out of nineteen cases.

Preferences for particular workers were based on the following attributes, ranked in order of the frequency with which they were mentioned by clients:

(1) informality (homely, easy to talk to),
(2) getting close enough for honest discussions,
(3) patience,
(4) equal caring for everyone in the family,
(5) politeness.

We have noted that clients chose factors relating to warmth of relationship and ethical integrity, and judged workers in these terms. Their regard for ethical factors and their relative disregard for efficiency in material matters were both underestimated by the caseworkers.

An attempt was made to examine relationships also in terms of clients' feelings of goodwill, confidence and affection for workers, and to discover how clients have manifested these feelings. Seven families demonstrated their feelings by acts of personal generosity to the Unit. These feelings appeared to be a response to the workers'

SUMMARY, CONCLUSIONS AND SUGGESTIONS

demonstrations of friendliness, rather than merely an expression of thanks for a professional service. In several cases, clients considered that these warm feelings were an end in themselves and outlasted any current or earlier circumstances of need or help. Some clients became, in various ways, contributors to service as well as receivers of it.

The caseworkers shared some important aspects of their private lives with seventeen families. (No family was wholly in ignorance of his worker's domestic situation.) Workers and clients deemed this knowledge to be positively helpful in ten cases, and harmful in none. But the importance of professional discretion in this kind of disclosure has been emphasized.

6 *Authority* Workers exercised firmness and set limits in work with twenty-three families. This seemed to be compatible with close relationships, and with the clients' identification with workers. Long-term resentment was not increased through this exercise of authority. Five families emphasized the setting of limits as a valuable aspect of help. Clients did not appear to expect workers to permit total freedom in behaviour.

Several clients condemned scroungers and others who misuse the Unit's services. The limits that some clients wished to set on help were more rigorous than those set by caseworkers, and certainly as moral.

At least five clients managed clearly to describe the concept of empathy in speaking of their social workers' relationships. By contrast, official relationships were seen as slow, interfering (giving advice rather than guidance), and impatient.

7 *Good and successful work* The extent to which workers ally or separate the notions of good work and successful work has been described. Good work appears to be seen in terms of the ethical input of the worker; successful work was more usually judged by changes in the social functioning of the client. 'Success' was regarded with suspicion by workers who were especially alive to the possibilities of manipulating behaviour unscrupulously and without the consent and comprehension of clients.

With regard to the outcome of work, the Unit's 'success' was most apparent in those areas of social functioning which the workers had previously designated as their clients' most pressing emotional needs (irrespective of the precise form of the referral problems). This looks like a self-fulfilling prophecy, but any such element was entirely unwitting. The areas most changed were those relating to a client's performance as parent or spouse, his coping with inner feelings of distress, and his response to the stress of external unexpected events. Financial management, changes in

SUMMARY, CONCLUSIONS AND SUGGESTIONS

children's behaviour, and changes in the work-habits of the father showed less change. It seems possible that the quality of relationships established by the Unit's workers was particularly effective in helping clients with malfunctioning in personal relationships arising from feelings of confusion, low self-esteem, anxiety and panic; but was less effective in other aspects of social role-performance, even where the latter were integral with the referral problem.

8 *Sub-groupings* Certain findings were discussed from a consideration of the following sub-groupings:

unsupported mothers,
clients who have worked with only one caseworker,
clients in very long contact,
open and closed cases.

Two basic theoretical matters have been considered relating to the nature of professional relationships in social work. It has been suggested, first, that, with clients whose problems are multiple, or who appear to lack integration in some areas of personality, the consistency and even tenor usually associated with professional relationships may be inappropriate. Only at a very fundamental level of caring was it possible to detect the common element which linked together the very broad ranges of service, help and relationships offered by some workers to some families.

Secondly, the work of the Sheffield FSU has suggested very strongly that in some cases the professional task of casework —certainly an anti-professional task in the light of some notions of professionalism—is to overcome the cognitive and emotional distances between workers and clients who, left to their own spontaneous goodwill and responsiveness, would fail to overcome them. In this study, reciprocity in relationships was often presented by workers and clients as fundamental to effective casework. Moreover, workers were often active helpers in precisely the same way that friends would be active. Equality (respect, not giving advice) was emphasized.

Yet the caseworkers were friends *with power*—more than friends in the views of some clients, better than family and neighbours in the views of several more. They exercised power not only on behalf of clients but also within the lives of clients; their power was perceived not as arbitrary and unpredictable (like official power) but as consistent and exercised in the context both of true friendship and of professional caring.

Both the exercise of power and the professional caring seemed to have become acceptable to clients first because they received initial

SUMMARY, CONCLUSIONS AND SUGGESTIONS

help in the mode in which they requested it. Usually this involved immediate material aid, but aid which, it is suggested, held symbolic as well as objective and short-term significance.

Reference has been made to the influence of flexible administration, and the availability via caseworkers of immediate and relevant service, as significant in the Unit's popularity among its families.

Consequential hypotheses about the practice of family casework

Referral (1) Clients referred by other clients have more realistic expectations than those referred by other services.
 (2) Inadequately prepared clients base their expectations either on their experiences of other services or on projections of their own needs.
 (3) The presence of services, and even direct contact with a service, does not indicate that this help is regarded as available or acceptable by the client.
 (4) Ambiguity in the client-role, when a client is in touch with more than one service, leads to the splitting of his ambivalence about seeking help. As a result, feelings towards different workers or agencies contain irrational additions of extreme goodwill or ill-will, irrespective of the actual performance of worker or agency.
 (5) This irrational component may be exacerbated by the collusion of the social workers involved. Thus, a spiral develops of dependence—ambivalence—splitting—goodwill/ill-will—intensification of unmet needs—increased dependence—increased ambivalence ...

Help at referral and subsequently (6) Material need and material help sometimes have symbolic qualities, indicating the presence of other needs and the willingness to offer other help.
 (7) Clients remember most clearly the help they receive in a crisis.
 (8) Clients' awareness of the quality of material help extends into their assessment of other kinds of help.
 (9) The distinction among caseworkers between professional relationships and befriending, though useful, overlooks the fact that clients do not draw the distinction in the same way.
 (10) The model of relationship regarded by the caseworker as the day-to-day norm of practice affects the attitudes of clients to the service received, and predetermines which areas of clients' attitudes and capacities will be changed.

SUMMARY, CONCLUSIONS AND SUGGESTIONS

(11) The kinds of relationship presupposed in professional help and befriending are not mutually exclusive.

(12) The home visit and agency-based interview are not acceptable to or useful with clients who seek to establish their physical or moral domination in their families.

Discussions between workers and clients (13) Even when a wife's health and feelings are not specifically mentioned as referral problems, they will form a major area of discussion with a large and needy family.

Memories and recollections of clients and workers (14) (a) These diverge, irrespective of closeness and intimacy in relationships.

(b) The less the intimacy, the greater the divergence.

Relationship factors (15) There is a positive relationship between the extent of the client's identification with the values and objectives of the worker and the extent of changes in his social functioning.

(16) Clients relate most closely either to their first or last worker, or to the worker in longest contact with them.

(17) When clients invest feelings in their relationships with workers, these are perceived as ends in themselves, irrespective of needs and problems.

(18) Thus there may be a discrepancy between the client's wish to maintain a close friendship, and the worker's goal of client's independence.

(19) (a) The expression of authority in relationships is not in itself incompatible with warm feelings between client and worker, or with client's identification with worker.

(b) Clients do not expect or desire total permissiveness from social workers.

(c) The client's acceptance of a worker's authority depends on his perception of accurate empathy in the worker.

(20) Befriending-relationships are more effective against feelings of ineptitude, depression, and anxiety in family relationships than against failures in extra-familial role performance.

(21) (a) Following the closure of a case, the client's memory of facts does not decline significantly, but he recalls less vividly the feelings present in the relationship (in terms of both affection and authority).

(b) The social worker's recollection of both facts and feelings grows less vivid following the closure of a case.

Sub-groupings (22) Unsupported mothers do not, as a group, enter into closer personal relationships with individual case-

SUMMARY, CONCLUSIONS AND SUGGESTIONS

workers than other groups, but are more likely to identify with their values and standards.
(23) No special advantage in the quality of relationship or outcome of work accrues from avoiding changes of worker.
(24) The length of contact between client and agency does not affect the quality of relationships with the agency's workers.

Some factors which, in the views of clients or workers, indicate or lead to success in social work practice

A client's acceptance of an agency as helpful relates to the immediate meeting of needs in the manner presented.

Furthermore, the client judges the agency as successful if workers anticipate and provide help in areas other than those designated as referral needs.

Workers are deemed to be successful by clients if they appear to think about needs and help in the way the clients do, i.e. closing the cognitive gap. This does not mean that clients expect workers to 'talk the same language' or to do everything asked of them; reference has been made to the concept of empathy—the capacity of the worker, perceived by the client, to see and experience things in the same way as the client.

The client's awareness of this quality or skill in the worker is assisted by the worker's appropriate disclosures about his own life.

These comments relate closely to Mayer and Timms's findings (1970): that the satisfaction of the client is associated with a progression of activity; his material needs are dealt with early, and the worker enters the client's trust by leaving some of the initiative for work with the client and by responding to the client in ways perceived as meaningful and relevant.

The views of workers and clients with regard to successful outcomes of work will differ in so far as they tend to recollect the referral situation differently.

When an attempt is made to assess outcome by reference to changes in the client's social role performance, regard must be paid to the quality of relationship established by the worker, and to the possibility that all the necessary role-changes may not be compatible within the scope of one relationship.

Clients judge workers as successful if they are both at ease and caring in relationship, and are perceived as being ethically reliable.

SUMMARY, CONCLUSIONS AND SUGGESTIONS

Social workers associate these factors with 'good work' rather than 'successful work'.

These factors do not directly influence a client's role-performance outside the family, but may relate directly to intra-familial changes.

Clients usually equate good work with successful work. Social workers tend to separate the notions of 'good' and 'successful'. Some divorce them entirely.

When a client sees the worker-client relationship as having an intrinsic value (i.e. beyond the requirements of his problems and needs), his perceptions of purpose and success are related more to short-term achievements than to long-term goals of independent social functioning. If workers identify with clients in this situation, they may similarly judge their success by reference to short-term achievements; for friendly relationships tend to exclude consideration of long-term purpose, and intimacy promotes ambiguity in the notion of success.

In order that 'purpose' and 'success' should not be divorced from each other, it is necessary for social workers to retain, and to share with their clients, some long-term criteria for evaluating their work together.

Successful social work consists of the achievement of both long-term and short-term goals, and the awareness of their causal and experiential connectedness; the achievement and the awareness being present in the minds of both worker and client.

Notes

Several references were made in Chapter 1 to the dilemmas of defining purpose in social work practice and to the uneasy situation of practitioners, caught between theoretical exhortation and administrative demand and lacking within their profession an appreciable number of middle-range models and strategies for dealing with groups of problems. These models seemed at one time to be developing satisfactorily either, as Bartlett (1970) has shown, in relation to the socio-medical needs of certain categories of patient known to medical and psychiatric social workers, or in relation to the implementation of clearly defined statutory requirements as in the former Child Care Service. Recently difficulties arising from the loose ascriptions given to the word 'generic'—derived from education but inappropriately applied to practice, so as to form unimaginable entities like 'a generic social worker' and 'a generic caseload' (but not yet 'a generic client')—have combined

SUMMARY, CONCLUSIONS AND SUGGESTIONS

with the wish to improve services by extending them. The resultant dilemma has been stated, in terms of the administration and policies of social service departments, by Rodgers and Stevenson (1973 p. 333):

> The Seebohm Committee ... tempted social workers and administrators to continue to think in vague terms because of a fundamental weakness in its exposition of what the new department was to do, and why. Without the classification of function ... the inadequacies of the separate services as they existed in the old situation could not rationally be made good; without it, the brave vision of new and uncharted areas of welfare to be encompassed merely complicated further the difficult task of formulating policies to remedy past omissions.

The present study has attempted to add a little to what we know about what is perceived and experienced when social workers set out to help people. It offers little, if anything, to the task of formulating social policies, but has, I hope, some relevance beyond the work of the Sheffield Family Service Unit to the broader professional task of defining purpose, not on the basis of vague intention, but in the light of need and experience.

Appendices

Appendix I
Outline of guided interviews with the families

This represents the order of discussion for most interviews, and an approximation to the way in which questions were asked; but the order varied when respondents spontaneously introduced topics in a different way.

    What were the circumstances that led to your being in touch with the Unit?
    How had you tried to cope with things before that?
    Were you in touch with any other welfare people at that time? Did you talk it over with friends?
    What were you hoping the Unit might do?
    What did you expect they would be like?
    Did you think they came from the Town Hall? What about now?
    Who was the first person to visit you from the Unit?
    What did he/she do at the start? Was that what you wanted?
    Who has visited you since then? Can you remember their names? How long did each one work with you?
    How long have you been in touch with the Unit altogether?
    How often do/did they come to see you? Do you ever go to the Unit yourself? What for, particularly?
    Which worker did you like best? What was it about him/her? Why did you like him/her specially?
    When the Unit people visit you, what sort of things do you talk about?
    What do you talk about most?
    What have you disliked?
    Do you feel you could speak your mind?
    Could you try to recall the different ways in which the Unit have tried to help?
    If you could choose only one of these ways, which would you say has been the most helpful?

APPENDIX I

Has any of the workers ever done anything you disliked at the time? Or said anything?

You told me earlier that you were in touch at one time with (social agencies). Have you been in touch with any others? Do you feel that the Unit has helped the way you get on with them, or hasn't it made much difference?

What do you think makes a helpful social worker?

EITHER

Were you quite glad to finish your contact with the Unit?

OR

Supposing everything was sorted out all right, and you didn't have any more troubles—if your ship came in—would you be quite pleased not to need the Unit's help any more?

Have you been satisfied with the Unit, or has it sometimes been a waste of time?

If you had any friends with problems, would you recommend them to go to the Unit? For what sorts of problems particularly?

Appendix II
Schedule for interviews with the social workers

As in interviews with the families, those with the social workers were often preceded and accompanied by fairly wide-ranging discussion when this was spontaneously introduced by the social workers.

Name of family: Open/Closed
Name of FSU worker interviewed:

I Referral information

1. Were you the first worker in this case?   Yes/No
   If not, who was?
2. What were the referral difficulties as seen by the FSU worker at the time?
3. Was family in touch with other helpers (e.g. agencies and friends) at that time?   (name)
4. How had family tried to cope with referral difficulties before referral?
5. Who referred the family?
6. What was this family expecting the Unit to do?
7. What were they expecting the Unit to be like?
8. Did they know FSU is non-statutory?   Yes/No/Don't know
   If *No*, do they know now?   Yes/No/Don't know
9. What help was given initially?
                                            Material/Negotiating/Support
10. Was this what the family wanted at the time?
                                                     Yes/No/Not sure

APPENDIX II

II Worker–client relationships

11 How long were you (or have you been) in touch with this family on a regular basis?
12 How long was, or has the family been in touch with the Unit?
13 Who have been the Unit workers and students in this case, and for how long?
14 (a) Do you get the impression from the client that client has preferred one particular worker? If so, whom?
(b) In your view which worker has been most successful?
Why (a) ?
Why (b) ?
15 Has the family been able to speak their mind honestly to you?
Always/Usually/Don't know/Sometimes/
Probably not much
Has this been the case in relation to other Unit workers?
Probably/Don't know/Worse with..../Better with....
How many *specific* incidents can you recall of dishonest speech to yourself?/to other workers?
How many *specific* incidents can you recall of holding back important information to yourself?/to other workers?
16 What has been the frequency of visits?
17 What subjects are mentioned in visits?
Which subject is *most* discussed?
Are there any topics of discussion which you feel the clients *avoid* sharing with you?
18 Did you ever tell this family about your private life?
Yes/No
Did other workers with this family? *Yes/No*

III Helping

19 What kinds of help have been given (altogether)? (tick)
clothes
holiday/convalescence
club facilities
negotiating with other agencies
budgeting
emotional support
befriending
any others
20 Which one would *this family* regard as having been most helpful?
Which one would you regard as having been most helpful?

21 Has family been to the Unit?   Yes/No
    For what?
22 What is the quality of family's relationship with SBC?/with other services? (name)
    Has association with Unit changed these relationships?
    Which?   How?
23 Has this family ever referred another for help?
    If *Yes*, what kind of help?

IV Criteria of success

24 Do you personally feel you have (or, at close of case, had) the family's
    goodwill?
    confidence?
    affection?
    If *Yes*, how is this shown?
    If *No*, how is this shown?
25 Was there a significant turning point in this family's relationship with you?/or with the Unit?
26 What qualities of personality does this family
    expect to find in social workers generally?
    consider would make a good social worker?
27 If the answer to Question 18 was *Yes*, did telling the family about your private life assist your relationship or not?
    Yes/No/Don't know
    In what way?
28 Have you ever said/done anything which the family disliked/resented at the time?
29 Have you ever been *firm*   (tick as appropriate)
    in *instructing* the family to do something?
    in *advising them very strongly* to do something?
    in requiring certain *standards of behaviour*?
    in *discouraging certain kinds of talk*?
    in *not* telling the family what to do?
30 Have you set limits in other ways?
31 Of your being firm and/or setting limits, have these clients
    been glad in the long run?
    continued to resent?
    taken no notice?
    others?
32 What has the work with this family achieved?   (tick)
    Financial management   Better/Same/Worse
    Marital relationships   Better/Same/Worse
    Parent-child relationships   Better/Same/Worse

APPENDIX II

    Work attendance   Better/Same/Worse
    Children's behaviour generally   Better/Same/Worse
    Maintaining levels of *individual* competence
                                         Better/Same/Worse
    Coping with inner distress   Better/Same/Worse
    Coping with external distress   Better/Same/Worse

33 Effect of closing this case would be/has been that
    family continues to increase achievements
    family maintains level achieved
    family levels decline in some way
34 Was the family glad to finish with the Unit?
35 Was the case closed because 'successful'?
36 What in your view makes a 'good caseworker' and 'successful caseworker'?

Appendix III
The families interviewed

Mr and Mrs Abbott
Mr and Mrs Bailey
Mrs Charles (deserted by her husband)
Mr and Mrs Cooper
Mr and Mrs Dell
Mr and Mrs Dimmock
Mr and Mrs Ewart
Mr and Mrs Francis
Mr and Mrs Gordon
Mrs Harris (widowed)
Mr and Mrs Ilson
Mr and Mrs James
Mr and Mrs Kennedy
Mr and Mrs Lowe
Mr and Mrs Milward
Mr and Mrs Norris
Mrs Osborne (divorced)
Mrs Price (husband not present for interview)
Mr and Mrs Roberts
Mr and Mrs Sanders
Mr and Mrs Sheldon
Mrs Stocks (husband in prison)
Mrs Tyson (widowed)
Mrs Underwood (husband not present for interview)
Mr and Mrs Vincent
Mrs Williams (husband not present for interview)
Mrs Yates (widowed)

In this list four partnerships were cohabitations following the breakdown of the wife's first marriage, and were known to their neighbours as Mr X and Mrs Y, not as Mr and Mrs X as recorded here.

Appendix IV
Major subjects discussed in interviews

Family	Content of discussion remembered by family	Additional topics recalled by worker	Additions from records
Abbott	children affairs connected with money recent events at home	wife's health	
Bailey	money matters	children's health marital tensions the care of the home	
Cooper	money matters the worker's life	marriage husband's work	care of children
Charles	wife's feelings daily events	care of children	
Dell	money matters wife's health any recent marital difficulty	care of children husband's health husband's offences	
Dimmock	(everything)	wife's health care of children money matters behaviour of wife's relatives	marital tensions contraception
Ewart	(everything)	care of children school attendance money matters marital problems drinking unemployment	

APPENDIX IV

Family	Content of discussion remembered by family	Additional topics recalled by worker	Additions from records
Francis	(everything)	money matters marital problems wife's feelings of depression	
Gordon	care of children conversation on daily events men the wife's health housing		marital problems husband employment money matters
Harris	money matters old times	children's school attendance	
Ilson	wife's younger days wife's health and feelings worker's recent life	marital interaction care of children housekeeping	contraception
James	any immediate crisis money matters (everything else)	behaviour of daughter marital tensions	other children's behaviour rehousing contraception wife's health
Kennedy	money matters wife's feelings	children's behaviour marital tensions contraception/sterilization	husband's health and work
Lowe	money matters wife's feelings worker's feelings	wife's relatives wife's health children's school attendance	
Milward	wife's feelings family's health money matters	marital tensions	care of children
Norris	money matters	wife's health children's behaviour	marital tensions

APPENDIX IV

Family	Content of discussion remembered by family	Additional topics recalled by worker	Additions from records
Osborne	daily events husband's behaviour and work children's behaviour wife's feelings		
Price	money matters care of children marital tensions wife's feelings		
Roberts	money matters daily events		
Sanders	family life marital tensions husband's hobbies wife's feelings	money matters husband's work	
Sheldon	money matters husband's health	care of the house marital tensions	contraception care of the children husband's imprisonment
Stocks	money matters wife's feelings	care of the house	contraception marital tensions wife's health
Tyson	money matters wife's health wife's feelings	children's behaviour husband's death overcrowding	
Underwood	daily events care of children marital tensions any special crises		
Vincent	money matters problems with the authorities client's need for self-confidence	husband's unemployment marital tensions care of children	

APPENDIX IV

Family	Content of discussion remembered by family	Additional topics recalled by worker	Additions from records
Williams	care of children money matters any special crises	husband's unemployment marital tensions	
Yates	wife's feelings care of children	relationship problems with men	

Appendix V
Recollections of the length of contact

Family	Clients' assessment of length of contact	Workers' assessment
Abbott	accurate	underestimated 7 months
Bailey	accurate in all, but exaggerated the contact of the preferred worker by 6 months	underestimated 6 months
Cooper	underestimated 6 months (one permanent worker only)	accurate
Charles	overestimated 1 year (by exaggerating length of contact of current (favourite) worker)	overestimated 1 year
	This is a close relationship with considerable dependency from the client	
Dell	(couldn't remember—this is a crisis-ridden family)	accurate
Dimmock	accurate	accurate
Ewart	overestimated 1½ years: a drifting and crisis-ridden family	accurate
Francis	accurate	accurate
Gordon	underestimated 2 months	underestimated 5 months
Harris	overestimated 3 years (in fact, a 10 year contact, off and on); but showed remarkable accuracy in recalling the order of social workers	underestimated 6 months

APPENDIX V

Family	Clients' assessment of length of contact	Workers' assessment
Ilson	underestimated 1 year (a very dependent relationship)	accurate
James	accurate	accurate
Kennedy	overestimated 1 year (exaggerated length of contact of the first worker)	accurate
Lowe	overestimated 1 year (exaggerated contact with first—and favourite—worker who helped with the major crises)	underestimated 1 year
Milward	overestimated 1 year (in a 7-year contact)	underestimated 2 years
Norris	accurate	overestimated 1 year (regarded as a demanding case)
Osborne	not sure. A very confused and depressed woman, whose accuracy of memory extends only to the current worker	overestimated 1 year (regarded as an emotionally demanding case)
Price	overestimated 2 years (a very close relationship with only one permanent worker)	accurate
Roberts	accurate	overestimated 8 months
Sanders	overestimated 1½ years (out of a 5½ year contact)	accurate
Sheldon	accurate	underestimated 6 months
Stocks	accurate	underestimated 1 year
Tyson	overestimated 3 years (very close relationship with one worker only)	accurate
Underwood	overestimated 1 year (very close relationship with one worker only)	accurate

APPENDIX V

Family	Clients' assessment of length of contact	Workers' assessment
Vincent	overestimated 2½ years, but accurately recalled the length of contact with their favourite worker. Exaggerated time with previous worker at a period of great family crisis	underestimated 6 months
Williams	overestimated 2½ years (exaggerated the contact with their favourite worker)	underestimated 8 months
Yates	overestimated 1 year 4 months, (exaggerated contact with present worker, with whom she has a very close relationship)	accurate

Appendix VI
Selected transcriptions from the interviews with families

The following extracts are of two kinds: the first group provide additional brief examples of clients' recollections of their experiences, and of their perceptions of certain attributes in the social workers; the second give longer and more general impressions of typical study interviews. In these extracts w refers to wife, H to husband, I to interviewer.

Brief Extracts

Examples of stress at the time of referral, vividly recollected in the present

(i)

w I phoned her up at the office because I had tried all over to get this electricity light bill paid and nobody would help to pay it and I could not borrow the money and I got in touch with [a social worker] and she came out. The electric light man said 'Don't worry love because you will only have it off for tonight; get in touch with the Children's Department in the morning'. But she came out and asked how much it was—it was £12. And she asked me if I had anything towards it but I said that we could not manage on what we were getting now. Nobody told us that we could go to the assistance and get our rent money and our money made up. We were living on £7 odd a week and paying £2 10s a week rent out of it and £2 for coal and nobody told us. Any rate, *she* did not tell us—she never said anything about the money we were getting and I asked her if she could do anything about the electric light bill; could she lend us the money and we could pay her a little bit each week when his money came? She said No it was up to the Children's Department and we had to wait until they had a meeting.

APPENDIX VI

... Now with Pat—she has been right different. I was due to have the baby, and my husband got into trouble because we had nowt again at Christmas. And they told me when I had the last one I wasn't to have any more because I would not live to see a third. But while Pat was coming to the house I did well because she took me to the doctors and all over because I would not be examined and messed about and she wanted me to go. And she took me in the van and the doctors said I had lost it, (it was not very far on), but when I got caught with this one, she was right worried about me. I was not really worried because we wanted it. But when it got to the end, I got these breathless turns, and she came the week before Christmas because she knew we had got nowt. We had got no Christmas dinner, nothing, and she came on the Wednesday and he had gone out and I was upset. She asked me what was up. I wouldn't tell her that he had gone out looking for something to do [i.e. to steal] because.... I said we had got nothing and with these breathless turns I was frightened to go into labour in case I won't come out of it. I thought I was dying. Everything got me down. He done a job [i.e. theft] at Christmas and we got over Christmas and New Year and then I won £50, and then the police came for him and took him away and I was left over the weekend with the two kids. As it happened I had a decent neighbour that took the kids off me and this neighbour says to me why don't you phone Pat but I did not know her home number then, I only knew her office number. I got her on Monday dinnertime and she asked me what he'd done; and I said she would have to come out and I would explain it to her. And she came out and she went everywhere with me that day—probation office, and she phoned for me. They would not let him out all the time, and we had to go to court again. A friend went with me and I said I could not be in court this week. Pat said he will be coming home. She said if he was not home and I went into labour, she would come to the hospital with me and stay while I had the baby. She was really smashing. The only thing that got me mad and I was going to Downing Street over it—we were both working; well, I had trouble with my kidneys over having the baby so I had to give up. These two weren't at school or anything. Well, I asked Pat and the Probation Officer to save my husband from having to pack his job up. Could they try and get the children in the nursery up the road, because I could not cope with them all day as I was liable to pass out all the time. I said I could manage a couple of hours in a morning and then in

APPENDIX VI

the evening, until he comes home and gets them to bed. Anyway she said she had tried but they never got them in. But yet they took him to prison on a Tuesday dinner-time; Pat brought me home in a taxi from the court because you can imagine the state I was in and she left me with a neighbour while she went off somewhere else and she came back because she was going to put the kids in a hostel all night. I told her 'you are not taking them away'. Anyway she left them with me as long as I could pull myself round. But on the Wednesday morning my kids were in a nursery, I had a home help, free dinners and a houseful of furniture. The only thing I have never forgotten them for. I was pleased I got the help but, as I told Pat (and she says it was a pity), it was last August when I asked for this help because he had been leaving his job—all I wanted was the children in the nursery and he could have carried on working. He had to pack his job up to look after me and the kids, and that was why we had not got anything in. It was my fault really because I felt so bad, I thought I was dying and I kept telling him that I wanted the kids looking after.

H Of course we have realized our mistake since.
W There was this copper—he was definitely after him getting time, because he told me. He came up to the house and told me when he was away. He said I had better get used to being on my own and having the baby on my own—I would just have to get used to it. The Probation Officer was away that week and Pat took me down to see her when she came back and we told her. She said that they would try and get him home, but they admitted that they thought he was going down when it came to the big court; but they had tried their best not to let him go. Anyway I went in the hospital on the Friday morning—Pat used to come on a Friday morning when I wasn't working. Just before she came, I started losing; but [a neighbour] said hang on, and she came before I went away. They [the Unit workers] used to come to the hospital every day, both of them; they were ever so good to me; they used to come and keep an eye on him [husband] in case he did anything while I was away. They left him money for bus fares and things, and seeing to the kids. As it happened, I was in labour on the Saturday and he was at the hospital all day. Well, this copper had been to see him to tell him that he had to be at the Crown Court on Tuesday and saying that he had done another job on the Saturday, and we had to get witnesses from the hospital to say that he was there all day. I was fuming. About two o'clock, and I thought they had kept

APPENDIX VI

him [at the police station] and she said they were going to keep him until after Easter because he had to see a psychiatrist before then. This psychiatrist had to see him about Wednesday, before he had to go to court on Tuesday, but he had been in Wakefield or somewhere. The Probation Officer got in touch with his wife while he [the psychiatrist] was in court and got to know where he was, and Pat chased him up and phoned him and he said he would get the report in by Friday when he had seen him on the Wednesday. And anyway we managed that and never heard no more, thank God.

(ii)

I   How was it that you were in touch with the Unit?
W I was expecting his first child and the little girl was knocked down and killed. They needed a daddy. I didn't get a grant, you know like these maternity benefits, because with being separated I thought my husband would find out.
I   Your husband did not know where you were?
W No, you see we're not divorced and I thought they would catch me when claiming for the benefit. It was only £5 per week to live on for food and clothing for three children.... £15 he got for a wage, £12 went on mortgage, £5 on coal for warmth because the little girl was suffering from asthma. I got on to school, to ask for help because the little lad got out of control. Education asked me why he was like this and how long he'd been like this. It is only this past year he had got like this, I can't do anything for him. I've smacked him too much, and picked brushes up to him and he's making me a nervous wreck. So he said I'll put you on to the Child Guidance if you want. I said Yes, so long as I get these problems sorted out. The head teacher asked me how I'd got all my problems about money. Patrick was missing the things he was used to and he didn't understand about bills.
I   How old was Patrick?
W Patrick was four-and-a-half years old. He'd just started school.
I   It was difficult for him to understand?
W He was shocking. Well, I went to Child Guidance and they said he weren't bad enough to go to them. Anyway, I had a word with the head teacher—is there any way he could help me? I can't manage the clothing: I've got the other lad just starting school; it's too much for me. So he said I know a place [a social agency]. So I went there and the things they offered were rags—really too bad and smelly and I said I wouldn't put them on a dog. I said I wasn't having them. I'll wash out every night if I have to. So I went to jumble sales

instead. I told the Education that I have a maintenance order for the two boys but I didn't want to take it up because their father would always be on the doorstep. I then took a job at £6. What with paying £2 for someone to look after the girl and bus fares, it wasn't worth me working. I'd got nothing. I couldn't keep up with the children's clothes and so I asked the school doctor that they be put away until I got on my feet. I was having trouble with Mr A [cohabitee]. He did his best but it wasn't his mistake. I was shoving it on him, you know. He got furniture, and he went in and paid £400 deposit on this house—that were his savings. We didn't keep any secrets from each other. I'd come from Halifax; I was fed up with Halifax. I had the family round me all the time [i.e. her mother and sisters] but I would not let them do anything for me. When my mother did want to do anything for me, I always remembered that she hadn't wanted me to marry the man I'd married—she'd always said 'Don't come back to me'. And me sister—she offered me bits and things; but I said 'No, I'd made my bed, and I'd lie on it'. Anyway, I saw the school doctor and had a word with him: I were really a nervous wreck. I said you'll have to do something—take the kids away till I get on my feet. It's just got so as I don't know which way to turn. The school doctor came and I told him I've never been to anyone before and I'm not *that* desperate. I've been to Social Security and they don't help you one bit. *There's* a man [i.e. Mr A] who's worked for ten years and they won't help him one little bit: I think it's terrible. When you think hard we've always worked in our family. Well, she [i.e. school doctor] said, 'Now don't worry about it; leave it with me, I'll get in touch with the Family Service Unit'. I said thanks very much, I would like.... I don't like asking for help, but if I can get help, I'll keep my children, I won't neglect them. Well, this young lady came to see me, from Family Service Unit; I told her my problems and she got in touch with Social Security, and they told her there were a lot of children worse off than mine. I told her—it's a waste of time—I can't get owt from anywhere. I keep washing things out, but they don't last for ever. So I said, look get me a room—anything—and I'll let the children go. They're leading an awful life—it's not good for *them*. It was breaking me; I could rough it but the children can't. Anyway, she [the FSU worker] said come down to the clothing store on Wednesday, and I'll come and fetch you—at half-past-nine, I think she **said**.

APPENDIX VI

(iii)

H   (speaking of the circumstances of his referral) That's the last job [theft] I've ever done. Up to then I wouldn't humble myself to nobody. What did I get out of it? I got my kid a duffle coat. They fined me £10 but I couldn't pay. I done three months for it, I done three months for it [starts sobbing]—because I defied them, I wouldn't pay the damn thing. One small thing I done wrong. There's more people done wrong than I bloody did. Only one thing done wrong in my lifetime—fifty-three bloody years. I've done nothing wrong.

(iv)

I   How did you first get in touch with the Unit?

W   A friend of mine told me to ring to see if anyone would call from the Unit. Then a Miss X came (she was very nice) and that's her who really helped me to get launched. I got a £40 loan through her and I paid it back a pound every week and she used to call every week to collect it.

H   I was out of work and we got this electric bill in and I could not afford to pay it. I offered to pay so much a week but they would not allow us. They came and switched it off and as I had one or two commitments, we were finding it difficult. A friend said that if we could get someone from the Family Service Unit to come and see us, they will most likely help you—like pay the debt off and we could pay them back so much a week. So we applied, like, and the next thing this Miss X came. She saw what the situation was, and then she told us that we should have to wait a month while the committee sat. The first committee meeting she went to, they told her that she would have to look into it. Any rate, the second meeting she went to, they granted it. So it was nine to ten weeks before we really got going, from the time she came.

I   You were without light?

H   Yes.

I   Did you get fed up with waiting?

W   Not really.

H   Oh no, because she was a good woman—she came and explained to us and we realized the situation she was in, we realized how much she was trying to help us. And some weeks she came twice a week, didn't she? Nothing was too much for her to do. She put herself out to do anything for you.

W   She had this bungalow of her own and when we started stripping in here, she said don't bother about paper, I have got so many rolls left over that you can have.

APPENDIX VI

I   She was a generous person?
H/W Yes.
W   I liked her company, and I liked to talk to her. I used to tease with her, and I have done with the others who have come.

Examples of the use of firm support. Social workers seen as friends with power

(i)
I   For which problems particularly would you recommend them?
W   Well, I think they're good at *everything*. I mean, there's a lot of people who don't know which way to turn—besides money problems, clothing for children, and—well, anybody who's sick, some people, a lot of people, don't really know about going to the doctor. They just carry on and carry on. Whereas if you've got a social worker like them [the Unit], who could *see* when you need help.... They'd say, 'Well, you'd better go to the doctor's.' There's a lot of people who don't go. I *know*, I've got like, sometimes, I don't bother going.

(ii)
I   What is it that makes her [the Unit worker] a good person?
W   She's right understanding and she's very forward. If you say something and she disagrees with you, she'll give you a straight answer. She won't hide it, you know, like the rest of them [other social workers] would. I don't really know how to explain it, but she's different from the rest. She doesn't agree with you all the time, and she doesn't believe you all the time. Some others believe everything you say, but not her. Many times we have a disagreement with each other—you know, like bringing the kids up, income, and one thing and another. We're *honest*: we're just like two sisters. She's very truthful. She always says right, you know—so much here, so much there.... Sometimes, I'll say 'Let's leave it [i.e. a repayment] this week'. But she says, 'No, that's not right'. Some other social workers will agree with you; but she says 'No!' She's very firm and that's what I like about her.
I   Has she ever made you cross?
W   No. We've had our disagreement, but then we've sat down and we've not gone away in a bad mood.... She never takes anything to heart.

(iii)
H   I am not sure whether she came from the Social Services or the Family Services but she was a social worker. She said that

APPENDIX VI

she would see what could be done for us and then Jim [the FSU worker] approached us and asked if I would like to pay £1 a week towards the bill so that when I got a certain amount together, they could see about our being reconnected. Jim went through with this and I must say he has been marvellous and I don't know what we should have done without him; I was getting very despondent, and Jim has just said to me 'Look now, we have got *so* much together—we are saving!'— I am sorry I cannot save more. Yes, he used to call on us and collect £1 from us every week for eighteen months, we only missed a couple. It was Jim's idea—a damned good idea. After twenty-three weeks we got £20 together and he asked me if *I* would like to go to the YEB to ask about being reconnected. I said it would be better coming from someone like himself who was in an official position. So Jim tried this, but got a negative reply. He tried Social Security and they said that if we could get the amount [£98] split four ways it might help. It was Jim's idea that I should pay a quarter, Social Security a quarter, FSU a quarter and SSAFA a quarter. I thought it was marvellous, but this was August last year and still no verification from anyone, apart from Social Security. Jim said he would contact SSAFA and they sent £50 which was very good—this only left £50 and Social Security would not entertain it and this was very disappointing. This was disappointing because, after the £100, they wanted to charge another £16 for reconnecting. I was getting despondent. FSU said they would loan us so much and this was through the Children's Department. I agreed to pay back a weekly instalment of so much per week. We wanted a coin operated meter but they put us a quarterly meter in. They have taken one reading but we have not received a bill yet. Jim is collecting £1 a week from us—50p to be paid back to the Children's Department and 50p to be put by to accumulate for the bill. He is not one who rushes in, collects his £1 and goes. He is interested in us as people, he is interested in us as a family. He kept at me; at one time I could not be bothered. I was not interested, I had had just about enough, but Jim pushed me and he really made me interested in other things.

(iv)
H The only ones who could help us beside them were the Probation Officers. I'd been on probation, but I wasn't on probation then.
I So you had no reason for going to them?
H No, but all the same, if you're in trouble or not, you're

supposed to be able to go to them. But I can't seem to get on with, because [pause] you need something that's more sociable to visit. Well, you go to them places, and they're all official at you. The Unit's not official, it's more sociable. The people there have got sociability; they're out to help you—they can talk to highest or lowest—they're not lacking in sociability ... [pause] ... I can't explain it properly ... they're straightforward. Kay's like that, straightforward; you know, she takes some stick off me, because [he laughs] I'm always getting at her [i.e. pulling her leg, making jokes at her expense]. But she turns a blind eye. She is *good*. They've got sociability because they can understand us. They can understand us, them people, because they *want* to understand us. Do you know what I mean? We can talk to her about most problems, and she'll try to find out the solution. It's clever. For example, we got into debt with gas and light, and she worked out for us that we could pay 50p a week. Well, it was my fault—I had money but I was just too lazy to pay it. But we're all right now—I'm not in trouble or owt like that. We always pay our 50p a week.

W Kay used to come every week. We got into trouble with our rent, and to make sure we paid it, she used to come every week, and she'd take it *for* us you see.

H She was the *one* social worker who could tell *me* what to do [laughs]. She'd come and get fresh with me to make me do it, you know [laughs]. She wasn't snooty; she'd ask me in a certain way—when a person asks me to do a certain thing, then I'll do it. But if they *tell* me, that's authority, and I won't.... Like I said, it's attitude; and sociability mixed. It's attitude, and Kay's got it. In fact, most of the Unit's people's got it. Attitude and sociability, mixed. If someone says 'You've got to do this' or 'You've got to do that', then you don't do it. But if they say 'If you do this, it'll work out like that in the long run', then you do it.

I They explain it to you?

H Yes, they don't give us orders. They *ask* us, they *ask* us to do a thing in *this* way, you'll be better off than if you pay it *that* way. They ask you—in a roundabout way—but they ask you, and you do it. They ask you in such a way that it's a pleasure to do it for them. I can't explain myself—they ask you instead of telling you. They work it out and show us [i.e. in relation to budgeting a debt]. They explain every twist. They ask us to do it. When a person asks us ... it's different, asking, from telling a person. I can't explain myself. Yes, well, take when I was up for attempted murder—when were that?

APPENDIX VI

w Two years, or three years.
h Yes, three years since. Kay were there. That Kay were the only person who I walked out of court [with]. What did the barrister tip me for? barrister tipped me for ten years. Solicitor outside told me and the barrister that she's more help than my own wife. They'll listen to her more than anybody else. Her word has more weight, more authority....

(v)
w They never let you feel as if you are poor—they never let you think that you are poor. They make you feel as if you are just talking to a neighbour or a friend.
h You are never frightened when they are coming. They don't treat you like that.
w When you go up there to see them and you have to wait.... Now some places don't care how long you wait; but there, they bring you a cup of coffee and ask how you are. When they come out after you have been kept waiting, through no fault of their own, they say they are sorry.
h Put it this way, if I was in trouble, like with my rent, I would rather go up there and see them than go to the Town Hall, they make you feel frightened—shout at you.
w They [the Town Hall] make you feel as if you are a nobody; they make you feel like scuff, I'll put it that way. I have been in tears once or twice when I have come out of that place [the Town Hall].

(vi)
w Her from the Town Hall just used to come and then she was off again [i.e. didn't stay]; whereas the Unit are more *social* workers, they don't hurry you up all in five minutes, you know.
h They sit down and have a proper chat.
w They pop in for half-an-hour, so that you really have a chance to start talking. They've never been in a hurry. We've had time to talk in confidence with them; they don't just collect money and off, you know. They'll sit down and have a cup of coffee.... Well, when I won a bit, I gave the Unit £3. But really we got it back again with the things they gave us. They didn't want to take it, but I said to them—I've been glad of the help, and here's something for you. It's marvellous what they do to help you.
h And it's voluntary financed, isn't it?
i Yes.
w I wish we could give them more. Because they do do a hell of a lot for families. Well, the time they spend on us alone. And they even come in their spare time—in the evenings.

APPENDIX VI

Examples of clients' opinions about acceptable attitudes in social workers

(i)
w   They don't hold things against you. They treat you as if you were ordinary, if you know what I mean. They're like friends. If I feel bad, I know I can phone her up. She's closer to me than anyone else in my life. They're all like a family to me, closer than a family.

(ii)
w   We talk about everything—just like neighbours.
h   She's like a social worker. She's not snobbish or stand-offish. We'd have been in worse and worse without them. Since we got to know them, we've been better and better. Without them, like, we couldn't have survived.
w   Things are better in our ordinary life as well as with the debts.

(iii)
w   I used to put the kettle on and make tea. I used to take ages to get going when I was ill. I am better now, as you can see. Sometimes I felt I could not bear to tell them how I was feeling. They probably thought I was kidding anyway. It was so complicated here at times, I felt they would not believe it. Then she would start talking and we would chat things over. Then as she started talking she'd wriggle her way through [i.e. get through to me] and then we were all right. Some days I used to be 'off', you know, and not talk very much. It's easy if they're not too snobbish. Sometimes people with posh accents puts people off *straightaway*. I know. You can talk properly but when you hear them [workers] talking like that, it puts whoever it is right off ... at least until you get to know them after a few visits, you find they are not too bad and then you can start talking. [About another Unit worker] Yes, I have seen him a couple of times and I went one time and he gave me a right dressing down; but he *cared*, you know what I mean. He's so young. I hate anybody to grow old before their time. I would have loved to be able to work. I'd love to have been able to work at something like this [social work]. I have them [neighbours] coming here a lot with their problems. I learned a lot [about it] through having you lot [the Unit]. I'm not saying I'm very good, but I try to help, and I like talking.

APPENDIX VI

(iv)

I   Of all the visitors you've had, can you choose one who's your favourite?

W   Well, no. I don't think that's quite fair is it? But ... you see ... for myself I like all the *women* that come—I'm interested in women, you know, and like women. But the one man that I did like was him that left—that left to get married. And he'd just started to get used to us, like a family, you know, he used to come and bring his dog, and he'd sit with us until eight or nine o'clock at night sometimes to have a chat. Then he said he was going away to get married; and our two [children] were just getting used to him and getting his confidence: and he was getting used to our Andrew, getting him back on his feet again—with trusting people—when he had to leave ...

I   You've not been seeing so much of the Unit lately; supposing they stopped coming altogether?

W   Oh, I should be sorry. Yes, I would.... Because we don't go out such a lot, I really ought to be out working, but my doctor won't let me go. But—oh yes, I think it's nice.... It's been nice to meet them. And, you know, I think they do good work, actually.... They make you feel that you know somebody in the world, and you ... you're not *isolated*, you know. I think they're a good body of people altogether, I think they do good work.

(v)

I   Of all the things that they tried to do to help, which would you regard as the most helpful thing?

W   Well, not particularly helpful, but an instance: that Mr Young [the FSU worker]—you know, when my husband were coming out of prison, he *walked* from the ABC cinema to Browns Works trying to get a job for my husband to come out to, and he finally got one at Browns, for him to start. And that sticks in my mind. Not really *helpful*, but ... well, helpful, yes, because it got him a job, but.... [pause] Good, yes. For anybody to ... he'd never *seen* my husband, except ... well, it was after that that he went to prison to see my husband, you know, and he *didn't even know him*. And yet he did *that* for him.

(vi)

I   How would you describe him as a person?

W   Well, if you go off on the wrong track, and we tell him, then he speaks to him [husband], and then that gets us right.... I think he's smashing.

H   Mr Brown [an earlier worker] *tried* to understand you; but

APPENDIX VI

then he'd leave you with the thoughts what he thought himself. But not Mr Jones. Mr Jones will talk to you and leave you, and then he'll *come again* to see you, and ask you if you'd got over what you'd done.... But Mr Brown would come once a week and would tell you what to do, and then *off* [i.e. he didn't come back to check up how things were].... But not Mr Jones, he's a man who [shrugs, at a loss for words] ...

I Is he more interested?
H Ay, he bloody is [great emphasis].
W He's a digger. If you ask him, he'll dig deep down into it ...
I How would you describe a good social worker then?
W Understands, thoughtful.
H A man who's not afraid to walk into a house. He takes what he sees [i.e. accepts you as you are]. He sits with you and enjoys your company. He has a cup of tea. And when he walks out, he turns round and says 'I'm pleased to see you: I'll see you again next week'. But Mr Coates was the *best* of the lot [said twice and very emphatically].
I Why was he the best?
W If you hadn't got no money and they wouldn't help at Social Security, you only had to tell him and, by God, he'd see to them.
I He stood up for you?
W He did.
[H agrees]
W He had them [Social Security] in tears one day.

(vii)
I Looking back on all those you've met, which did you like most?
W Little Linda, because she had a sweet face ... she was warm and open and friendly in everything and in every way. She had some lovely attitudes. If I wanted to go to the Assistance Board, and they gave me short on my money, she'd be gentle and calm, get my money through, and that was it.
I You liked her best?
W Yes.
I Can you say just what it was about her?
W They've all been nice, but she's got a nice way of talking—nicely spoken—and she's been more, more like a sister to me—'cause she's been really good, you know, in her *soul*.
I How would you describe Linda to a stranger.
W Well, she wasn't easy—she was on the prim side. But she had a nice face. And I liked her hair,—right down [i.e. long]—black down. I said to her, 'Do you know, I wish I had hair like

APPENDIX VI

yours'. She said 'Do you?' So I said 'Yes, nice and long'. There was never anything out of place with her hair.

Longer extracts

(i)

I   How did you first get in touch with the Unit?
H   It was the Children's Department. We had difficulties. I hadn't worked for some time, and it got to be too much. We had periods when my wife felt she needed to get away; and at the time it was a question of whether or not we could have the children taken into care. So it was through the Children's Department that we first came into being, and that's how we went to Family Service Unit.
W   It's all right again now.
H   Yes. [He laughs] In the early days, she used to say 'What's he coming round here for?'
I   Did you have any idea what they were coming for?
W   I'd tried to do away with myself two or three times, and I thought they were just coming round to see—well, to keep an eye on me, and make sure I wasn't doing any harm to the children. There used to be a lady who came, and she was very nice, I really liked her. So when Brian came, it took me a long time to get used to the change.
I   Have you had just the two visitors?
H   No, there were one or two before.
W   But this lady and Brian were the main ones.
I   Can you tell me what you especially liked about this lady.
W   Well, she was [pause] she was a good listener; if you had something wrong, or if she could see you were upset, she'd sit down and take the trouble to find out what was the matter with you. She was very interested.
I   Did she do any practical things as well?
W   No, she didn't really do anything like that. She was just a good listener.
H   Yes, I wasn't home much at one time, I was mainly out working. And then in the last two years, what with the unemployment situation and then this coming up [i.e. wife's attempted suicide], it helped us her being available.
I   Have you had other visitors?
W   Yes, there was a man who came, but I couldn't seem to get on with him so well. I just used to sort of clam up when he came —I don't know if perhaps it was my fault, or his fault. I don't think it could have been my fault, because Brian says that, since he's been coming here, I've altered a tremendous lot.

APPENDIX VI

H   Yes, definite.
W   Definitely, haven't I?
H   She's altered a hell of a lot in the last two or three years. When she was upset, she used to tear through the house, and, you know, wash all the bedding and things like that. And, getting towards the end, I could sense it was coming to a climax again.
I   You've felt calmer since Brian's been visiting?
W   Yes.
I   Can you tell me how often the Unit have visited you?
W   Brian and Mary came once a week. The man came about once a month.
I   Why didn't you like the man as much as Mary and Brian?
W   He did seem [pause] he didn't seem so *warm*, somehow. He gave you the impression that it was just his job, and he wasn't really interested.
H   He gave you the impression that he majored in this subject at University, or something like that, without actually going into people's feelings.
W   Yes, and he just gave you, or he gave me, the impression that it was, well, his *job*; and he used to just sit there like.... Well, Mary and Brian, they'd bring *their* feelings into talking; but he'd just *sit* there, and say 'Nice day', and he'd leave it like that—*he'd* be sat over there, and *you'd* be sat over here. I'd make him a cup of tea—like I always do—and, well, that was it, sort of thing.
H   Now Mary next door [N.B. not the social worker], she's the sort of person who—well, when you're talking to her, you can tell that she's listening. She'd make a good social worker.
W   You see, if I don't take to a person straightaway, they might just as well not come no more. It's sort of impression I get that 'I can trust this person' or 'I can't trust this person'. And he was the sort of person—well, I couldn't quite trust him.
I   So it matters a lot, what a person seems like when they first arrive?
W   It does. I made my mind up as you were crossing the road.
H   Well, we had a Health Visitor this morning, and he was a bit like her ... trying to reassure us not to get despondent; we'd been cutting corners [i.e. economizing] and he said 'The only thing you can do is to cut corners!'
W   And I'd say to him—well, we'll starve if we cut corners any more than we are doing. We can't do the impossible: nobody can do the impossible.
H   Yesterday morning, we had another one, didn't we, from the Education Department. He was different again.... You know I

155

APPENDIX VI

was saying earlier about the difference between Brian and a University student. Well, you know, this one was different again—he was better educated [i.e. than the University student]—he had more of a grasp.

I A grasp of what?
H He seemed to understand more ... [he laughs]. I don't know how to classify it! He knew the *basic* things; he could see we were [pause] he could see the difficulties we were up against; he could classify different sorts of people [i.e. ? treat us relevantly].
W You know, I think if a person's homely.... Some people can be homely and another person can't, can they? You know what I mean? And if a person can't be ... can't go *into* a house.... I try to keep up a standard of living, but I can go in a lower house, with a lower class of people, and I can still be homely. And I can go into a home where people are supposed to have money; and I can still fit in with those.
H Be at ease, like.
I And this man yesterday, he was educated but homely with it?
W & H Yes.
W You've got to have this homeliness ...
H When you go to the Assistance ... you can go week after week, as we've had to do, and you see the same faces. And some of them complain because they've received the money too late to spend it in the pub at dinner-time. But another person can go in with a genuine thing [i.e. need] and they [SBC] say 'What do you want?' as if they'd spent all their sympathy on the earlier one who knows how to behave [sarcastically].
W The man who came yesterday more or less said all this, didn't he?
H Yes.
W You can somehow tell the genuine ones from the 'cheeky' ones ...
I How long have you been in touch with the Unit, over all?
W About five years.
H Yes.
I When they visit, what has the conversation been about?
W About the family, and anything interesting. For example, Brian will talk about plants, and things like that. His wife couldn't keep plants at one time, could she? But now she can [she giggles].... We talk about *ordinary everyday* things. And we talk about TV, what we liked about it and what we didn't like.
I And when he's talking like this—not about serious things or

APPENDIX VI

business things—do you sometimes think 'What's he wasting his time for?'
w Well, sometimes—only sometimes, mind you—I think to myself, 'You could be going to see someone a lot worse than what I am!' But then, two or three weeks later, I've gone *slowly* back towards where I was about five years ago, and then I'm pleased that he still comes. You see what I mean? Because he'll do *anything* for us, and he's someone you can tell *anything* to —as I have done *many* a time—and he'll sort of try to put me back on the right track. And more often than not he succeeds.

(ii)
I What happened that caused you to be in touch with the Unit?
w I went to the doctor's one day, and I hadn't got many friends, so I didn't.... I just wanted someone to talk to, someone to know how I felt.
I Were you feeling a bit depressed or something like that?
w Oh yes, that time, that particular October—something like that, I think; or November, I'm not quite sure. But it was after I'd taken the tablets. I took an overdose, and it was after I'd gone back home to my children and carried on from then— from taking the tablets—and tried to start again. I'd got to do it. I'd took the tablets once, and I've done that, and so ... I was here, I was alive, I was sent back home and was able to be with my children again. I hadn't had them taken off me. But I knew, I still knew what a struggle I had to face.
I How did you get in touch with the Unit? Did you know about them?
w The doctor knew about these people.
I So he sent you along?
w No. He rung up—there, while I was in the surgery. He says 'I know the kind of people for you, and they're marvellous people and they help you with your problems and help you to talk about them.'
I I see.
w I thought, if there was something like.... He says '*Honestly* they're marvellous.' I said 'Well, if there's someone like that, I mean, I'd like to come and see *you* every week, but, you know, if there's just someone to come and see—I can talk to about my problems.' It doesn't get you anywhere really, just talking to your friends. They did understand, one or two round where I lived: I used to go and talk to them, you know. It was still a struggle. Having someone who knows about things and families, this was what I wanted.

APPENDIX VI

I   When you first went to the Unit, or rang them up ...
W   Oh, it was a man that came to see me at first.
I   Who was the first one?
W   Oh, I was *really* down then. It were Mr Brown.
I   Oh yes, John Brown.
W   That's it, yes. I'd forgotten his first name. Yes, he was very nice.
I   What did you expect him to do—just sit and listen and have a talk?
W   Yes, he just listened, you know. After.... He helped me by *wanting* to talk. But afterwards it was the situation I was placed in, and being at this.... The thing that got me—I just kept getting upset about—was being on my own all day, you know. I couldn't seem to put my mind to do *work*, you know. I *did* it; all my house was straight and spotless. And having to get up in the morning, and take Amanda to school, and ... it was an effort. Oh, I was *so* low, you know, so *very* low, I wanted to do wonders, you know, for them [the children], yet it was a slow progress. This is it—anything slow, you know. But as I say things can't be done in haste.
I   No.
W   When I do things in haste, I regret sometimes.
I   We all do.
W   And this is it. When they're done in haste, you can't go back. And I've done a lot. I've done a lot of things like that; like walking out of my job.
I   Yes.
W   Even when I *like* a job.
I   But sometimes it gets you down and you walk out, is that it?
W   Yes. That is me. Yes.
I   A bit impulsive?
W   Yes, yes. And soon after Mr Brown was coming, he said he had to go and see another person—another family. So it wasn't.... He couldn't come any more. So he brought a new person along.
I   Who was that?
W   It was a ... [she starts looking through an old diary].
I   Man or woman, was it?
W   A woman—Oh dear, it's slipped my mind. It'll come to me—It'll come to me, long after you've gone.
I   Did she stay with you a long time?
W   Oh yes, yes. It'll.... She was.... Someone else was put in her place. She wasn't here long, the second one. She and her husband were leaving Sheffield to go and live in London; his job took him there, and that was the reason for her leaving the

APPENDIX VI

I   Unit. And she brought Jill along. She was permanent, Jill.
I   Yes.
W   It could have been since this time last year that Jill's been coming.
I   So Jill's been with you for about a year.
W   I'm not quite sure—I think so.
I   Yes. Looking back over all of them which did you like the best?
W   I didn't really get to know them all.
I   Not the ones in the middle?
W   John only came about four or five times, one day each week.
I   So it's been mostly Jill?
W   Yes. But the first one was here a long time. Oh, isn't it awful forgetting her name! I'm shocking.
I   Was it X, Y, Z?
W   She came from the north side of Sheffield ...
I   I can't remember all the names myself. But she and Jill have spent the longest time with you?
W   Yes. It's just *helped*—someone coming every week.
I   Which did you like better, do you think?
W   I liked them *all*—all the three girls seemed to ... they know their job, and actually they all had the same nature and everything. I couldn't say one was different from the other. I think, actually, they were like three sisters, you know, during the time I knew them.
I   Can you describe what it is that made you like them?
W   Yes. *Reassurance*—they give you. I feel a lot happier to have spoken to them and happier that they've come.
I   When they come, what sort of things do you talk about most? Is it about what's happening now, like your job, or is it more about memories of the past?
W   If I've seen the children.... No, it's not really going *back*; it's *everyday* happenings.
I   Just a chat?
W   Yes, just like that—over a cup of tea. What's happened, or perhaps, if I've seen my husband, and talk about my job, and perhaps what's been going on, you know. And perhaps if there *is* something, perhaps ask her advice, you know?
I   Yes.
W   But then she leaves the decision.... Perhaps she doesn't say anything—she leaves the decision up to me—what *I'm* going to do about it. They don't push you at all, you know. And I just talk about everyday things, you know—about going to my friend's house, or about how I've seen my husband. And then, when I was a bit upset about my job, and about the

APPENDIX VI

    letters I got from Social Security, you know, it just helps to ... [long pause] ...
I Do you ring them up sometimes when you feel you need them?
W Oh yes, I have, yes. And they've been there *straightaway*. That's been, you know [pause] ...
I That's something you like, is it?
W Yes, with having no-one to turn to.
I They come out at once.
W Yes. And I've called in at the Unit as well—if I've missed her [the worker]. Something perhaps has cropped up and I couldn't be in that morning. So I've gone the next day, even, just to see her, and to talk about me; or if I've had something on my mind.
I You just sometimes call in there?
W I've called in, yes, at Unit House, and she's been there, because I've missed her. Or for some reason, she hasn't made it when she says she *was* coming—on only one or two occasions.
I Yes. When the doctor first told you about them did you think they were Town Hall people—or did you know they were different from the Town Hall?
W I thought it was something to do with that.
I Something to do with the Town Hall?
W Yes. When he said 'Family Service, they help people with their broken homes and things like that,' the doctor said. He said, 'They *are* good people.' He rang them up and he said someone is coming to see you, a Mr Brown, next week, just like that! I said, I've been.... Oh, I told them [the children] about it soon after, that a Mr Brown was coming, and I said they're marvellous.
I You thought they were Town Hall people, did you?
W Only when I was in the doctor's surgery that time, and he put me in contact with them.
I Did you think they were going to be a bit different from the way they turned out?
W Yes. They didn't push you, or anything. When you tell them things, they're very patient and understanding. And, as I say, your life's your own, and it's what you make of it. But I am ... *me*. To keep me going and to feel tip-top, I always need someone to talk to. I've found this out myself. I've got to have this.... I've got to have these people who are trusting. I've got to have someone there all the time. Because I'm so lonely, I've always been a lonely person. I know there's others like me as well, so there's always someone—you always need a friend, don't you, to talk to?

APPENDIX VI

I   Everyone needs that.
W   And it does help—someone being there—I need that reassurance. To talk about.... That's why I talk about my job and *everything* that's happened every day. I don't want to brood on the past. I do tend to get like this—when I'm on my own, I think of the past. And I can't go back, I can't undo it. And if I get talking about the past, I can't keep the tears back.
I   No, I understand that.
W   And then, when *that* all comes out, I feel as if I need a cigarette and a tablet.
I   Yes, to calm you down.
W   'Cause I feel as though I'd ... I'd crack up.
I   Yes. I can see the way in which they help. By the sound of it you've felt you could be straight with them?
W   Oh yes. I feel as though I can with anyone; with married people.
I   Is it better if they're married people?
W   Yes, oh well, nearly everyone I come in contact with, they're all married—married men, and they understand. I like.... I don't know why.... I talk about my problems to them—and they understand—you see, they've got problems too.
I   Yes. In a way they know some of the feelings you've had?
W   They do, exactly, yes. But ... what can I do about it? How can I get myself out of this rut?—and not—I don't know—*think* about it, about my *past*.
I   The problem of trying to think about the *future*, isn't it?
W   Thinking about the future a bit more, and look on the bright side of it. It's still thoughts at the back of my mind which keep coming to the front, and trying to blot *this* out. This is what I'm trying to fight.
I   Yes.
W   And I can honestly say ... I'm ... I'm a bit of a pessimist.
I   Looking on the black side?
W   Looking on the black side. I'm *never* looking on the bright side.
I   Yes, you must have had rough times in the past.
W   I have, definitely. I can honestly say I *never* ... nothing seems to.... This is why I don't look on the bright side, because nothing *does* turn out. Nothing *ever* lasts; and I'm never happy for long. I'm always breaking down—crying here, you know; or after a day's work I come home crying. I've thought, 'I won't let my job upset me, I've got to be happy at my work, I've got to go to work.' This is what I've chosen to do, because the other thing I gave up because of the big responsibility preying on my mind of bringing the two children up—my own two. You know [pause], oh, I can give them *that*, true love

APPENDIX VI

and affection, but ... but also there's the ... you've got to.... It's more the *way* you bring them up. You've got to be firm with them. And I tend to be too easy-going; the children could play me up and it got topside of me; I couldn't keep them under control.

I Yes.

W So you've got to, perhaps, have a sharp tongue, and be firm with them, but [pause] ...

I But you're kind-hearted?

W Yes, too [pause] I've ... this is what even a few men have told me. I'm too ... I'm easy-going, and that [pause] ...

I Too kind?

W And too kind, and too ... you know; I wish I could be a bit more harder.

I Yes.

W Protect myself a bit more from the wolves.

I Yes. From what you've said, you'd like to keep in touch with the Unit people. Would you sometimes be glad to finish with them?

W Oh, no. I don't think I ever would. And ... unless perhaps the situation cropped up where I got married, and I was happy all over again.

I Yes.

W I don't think I'd, perhaps, have any more problems then, if I ... if someone understood, if my husband understood.

I Yes.

W It's just having that *someone* there—that *reassurance*.

I Are you in touch with any other social workers at all?

W No. No one, no one.

I And what about the Social Security?

W No, only when I come off work.

I I see.

W And they've got everything wrote down about my divorce, and my children, and my husband's got them [i.e. the children].

I So Jill never had to ring them up about anything?

W No. They asked, last time, 'If anything cropped up,' you know [i.e. another suicide attempt], 'Could we get in touch with anyone?' And I never thought of Jill. 'The last time, I was at a friend's house,' I said, 'but I don't go there now.' But [pause] ...

I Yes, so you could always ring Jill?

W So, I said, 'I ought to give you my friend's number, from the Service Unit; they call her Jill Burnett.' But I don't know her married name now. I know her as Jill Burnett, and I've forgot the number of her house. It's 39 ... I don't know it was ...

APPENDIX VI

I   I know the Unit House address.
W   So I ought to have given them the Family Service Unit. I know the street—but I left it—but if anything, perhaps, *did* happen, I ... as I say ... why I didn't give *that* address.... So I think you'd better leave that blank. Because I'm not.... There again, I wasn't looking on the black side, in case anything happened [i.e. I'm afraid to anticipate bad things in case they happen]. If anything did crop up like that, I don't know who to get in touch with, really. What near friend could I turn to? Because none of my friends are on the 'phone. So perhaps I always ought to keep Jill's [pause]....
I   Jill's 'phone number? Have you got the Unit's 'phone number?
W   No [discussion about address and 'phone number. She makes a note of them]. It's better to have it down [in the book]. It's safer. There again, I wasn't looking on the black side in case anything happened. Who to contact in case of emergency. So I'm not thinking about that. Well, actually I don't [think about emergencies]: it's some of the *other* things; family things, that I think about. It's silly, really. If I don't think about anything seriously, and who to contact.... If anything happens, to have to have your diary on you—they'd look through this, wouldn't they? Don't like to have too many names, though [she laughs].
I   You have to be careful whose names you carry about [laughs].
W   Don't you [laughs]? ... All these men friends, and all things like that [laughs]. It'd be a *right* case, wouldn't it [laughs]?!
I   If you had any friends who were in difficulties, would you recommend them to go to the Unit?
W   Yes.
I   Which problems in particular? [pause] Would it be problems like your own or problems like money or debts?
W   The Town Hall help you with all that, you know ... but ... [long pause].... I don't like to have a lot of payments on. I don't like that on my conscience, to borrow money.
I   No. But I wondered, if you had a friend who said to you one day, 'I've got so many debts and I don't know what to do,' would you think of the Unit?
W   I don't know about that. I don't know in what way they could help you, with me not having debts. I did a *little*— she did help me out—the other girl. I just borrowed some money to get something and I paid her back each week. Not to pay my debts off; the debts I've got in a rut with.
I   Would you recommend problems where people are feeling unhappy?
W   Yes. I don't know, you know; they just leave you to it—

APPENDIX VI

they just *hope* that it helps by them coming and listening, you know. You just ... as I say, you've just got to live your *own* life! But all the four years I was going with [i.e. courting] my husband, I used to live at their house at weekends. I used to see him every night, and he used to take me back home. I was never on my own then.

I   You'd like to get married again?
W   There again, I'm looking on the black side. I need a lot of luck, if it ever comes again. I don't know if it happens twice in a lifetime.

(iii)
I   Could you tell me how you came to be in touch with the Unit in the first place?
H   I was in prison.
W   Yes, and I got in touch with the Probation Officer, and he put us in touch with the Children's Department, and he said, would you like a social worker to call; because I've got no relations or anything like that, you know. So the next thing was, a social worker came, Sally—I've forgotten her second name—she's left now.
I   Did you have any idea what they'd be like?
W   Well, I thought they might be, you know, right 'upperty', you know what I mean?
I   A bit stuck up?
W   Yes. But when they did come they couldn't be more helpful, you know. They were right friendly, as though it were your relation, instead of a social worker.
I   You were expecting them to be a bit official?
W   Yes, and looking round, and all that, you know, to see what you do, and that. But no.... They said 'Well, come to the Unit', and.... Because when my daughter started school at first, she wouldn't go anywhere, and she wouldn't talk to anybody. But as soon as she went to family (SU) group, she sort of mingled with other children, and soon we were trying to get her to *stop* talking, you know what I mean?
I   Yes, that's good.
H   I went to prison because the light was out, you know. The electric bill, I were out of work. I had a bill and I couldn't pay it. I went out to see if I could get some more money like, you know, to pay it.
I   Yes.
H   We got it paid off. The Unit paid it, and we paid it back at so much a week back. Sally got it paid off; she paid it straightaway, like.

APPENDIX VI

I So you weren't in prison for very long?
H Six months
I As long as that?
H Yes ...
W It was William who visited us then. He's a Probation Officer now.
I Yes, that's right. Looking back on all those you've met, have you got a favourite one?
H Oh no, they've all been the same. They've all been helpful.
W They've all been the same, nice.
I Yes, I wondered whether there was something about them that...
W There was only the one I could *really* talk to though, and that's Sally. I've really felt comfortable with her. You could talk to *any* of them; but with Sally I could really tell my troubles, you know.
I What is it about her?
W Well, I don't know. She'll not let you, like, rabbit away—she'll ask you questions, you know, what I mean, not *personal* ones like, but.... How are you getting on? and Do you think this is upsetting you? and that sort of thing. She sort of goes *into* it with you. Whereas somebody else would just leave it at that.
I I see.
W I don't know how to put it. Do you know what I mean?
I She doesn't let you just rabbit on—she guides you?
W Yes, she gets a word in, like: you know what I mean.
I You *get* somewhere?
W Yes, because before I went into the Family Unit, I didn't speak to neighbours, did I, Bob? And I couldn't tell my troubles to next-door neighbours.
I Is that so?
H Not to *her* [i.e. neighbour]. We've no relations or anything like that.
W You know, it was like someone to talk to. When I went into the Family Service Unit group, they'd take the children, and the mothers would have a cup of tea. We were all in the same boat, you know what I mean—and you could tell your troubles.

(iv)
I If you were describing Linda [the FSU worker] to a friend, how would you describe her?
W She's sympathetic. She makes you laugh, which at times I needed very much. She's a happy person; in herself she's a happy person. She made you feel better when she was here. I

APPENDIX VI

    didn't see her too often *for myself*; but I met her a lot when she was with my mother. I saw her a lot then. To tell you the truth, when she came to see my mother, I though she was a bit nosey. She helped my mother in a different way, you see—not by giving her money, but by helping her to get her books straight and things like that, and I used to think it was *very* nosey. I remember once my mother lost her Family Allowance book, and Linda was looking all round for it, upstairs; I didn't like that a bit. But she wasn't like that with me.

I   Because it was a different problem?
w Yes; but then I was a lot younger then.
I   How often did Linda come and visit you?
w Well she only came a few times and then Hester came, once a week.
I   How long altogether were you in touch with Hester?
w For about two-and-a-half years. Nearly every week; it was very rare that she missed....
I   You've seen Linda and you've seen Hester. Is it possible to say which of the two of them you prefer?
w Oh, Hester [with great emphasis]. She's more of a friend. We're friends.
I   But obviously from what you've said you thought Linda was all right?
w Oh yes [with emphasis].
I   What is the extra thing that you feel Hester has got?
w I think it was because [pause] I was going to say it's because Hester's more my age; but she's not, Linda is pretty young as well. I think it's because we've got more in common. We used to talk about *her* as well as about *me*, and we used to get on ever so well together, and I really used to look forward to her coming.
I   When social workers visit you think it's helpful if they talk about themselves?
w Yes, it's got to be on a friendly basis with me; it's no good them coming to you and just sitting there like somebody not right [in the head] and listening to you and not caring a damn; you'd *know* that they don't. They don't *feel* for you. But when you get friends, you know, they feel for ... say, for instance, you get a black eye, they really feel it with you. I got that impression with Hester. You know, she used to hear me ... if, she saw me with a black eye, you felt as if she felt it as well.
I   Did she feel like a neighbour?
w Yes. No. Neighbours are no.... Not like neighbours. I don't

like neighbours. She was someone you know for a fact you could tell her a real dead secret and know she would keep it. You felt *safe* with Hester.

I You said earlier that your husband didn't like them coming. Does he still dislike it?

W He liked Hester, but he didn't like what she *was*. When he met Hester he was ever so friendly towards her; but I think it was because of my mother. He didn't like my mother. He said I was getting like my mother because I'd been in touch with these people; and I think he felt he couldn't bully me quite as much because I'd got these people. I don't think he liked that at all. I think he wanted me to have just him and nobody elese. He thought, you know, I'd got somebody else besides him.

I Did you feel that he didn't trust them?

W I don't really know. You see I've never talked about the Unit to him because he used to blow up. If I do anything like what my mother does, he doesn't like it.

I Are there any other ways in which Hester has tried to help? For example, clothes or help with the budgeting?

W No. She once tried to show me how to do my housekeeping—you know, money—but she didn't know the whole story [laughs]. I didn't tell her all about it. How she worked it out, I could do it easy; but she didn't know everything.

I So in things like money you didn't feel you could really use her?

W No, I didn't tell her about it because it didn't seem right at the time. I thought if I told Hester, she might *just* say something to my husband and he would get on to me when she'd gone. That happened once or twice. I said something about him to her, and I got a good hiding when she'd gone. This was then, not now. He wouldn't do it now. I've grown up a bit now.

I When the time came for you and Hester to say goodbye, were you glad?

W I don't know [pause]. I was glad that she thought that I was capable of carrying on on my own. I was glad about that. But there's been many a time when I've felt like getting in touch with Hester again, but I've managed to get through. But sometimes I wish Hester was still coming....

Bibliography

A comprehensive and illuminating bibliography and notes, directly relevant to studies of clients' perceptions of social work and social workers, are contained in Mayer and Timms's study *The Client Speaks*, published by Routledge & Kegan Paul, 1970. In the present study reference has been made to the following:

ASSUM, A. L. and LEVY, S. J. (1948), *Journal of Abnormal and Social Psychology*, 43, pp. 78-89.
BARTLETT, H. M. (1970), *A Common Base for Social Work Practice*, New York, National Association of Social Workers.
BASW (1970), *Research in Social Work*, Monograph no. 4, London, British Association of Social Workers.
BERGIN, A. E. (1963), *Journal of Counselling Psychology*, 10, pp. 244-55.
BERGIN, A. E. (1966), *Journal of Abnormal Psychology*, 71, pp. 235-46.
BLAINE, G. B. and MCARTHUR, C. C. (1958), 'What happened in therapy as seen by the patient and his psychiatrist', *Journal of Nervous and Mental Diseases*, 127, pp. 344-50.
BOTT, E. (1957), *Family and Social Network*, London, Tavistock Publications.
BREEDLOVE, J. L. (1972), in MULLEN, DUMPSON *et al.*
BROWN, G. E. (1968), *The Multi-Problem Dilemma*, New Jersey, Scarecrow Press, Inc.
BUTRYM, Z. (1968), *Medical Social Work in Action*, London, Bell.
CARKHUFF, R. and BERENSON, B. (1967), *Beyond Counselling and Psychotherapy*, New York, Holt Rinehart.
COFER, E. N. and CHANCE, E. (1950), *Journal of Psychology*, 29, pp. 219-24.
DOCKAR-DRYSDALE, B. (1973), *Consultation in Child Care*, London, Longmans.
EYSENCK, H. J. (1952), 'The effects of psychotherapy—an evaluation', *Journal of Consulting Psychology*, 16, pp. 319-24.
GEORGE, V. and WILDING, P. (1972), *Motherless Families*, London, Routledge & Kegan Paul.
GOLDBERG, E. M. (1970), *Helping the Aged*, London, Allen & Unwin.
GOLDRING, P. (1973), *Friend of the Family*, Newton Abbot, David & Charles; also New York, Harper & Row.

BIBLIOGRAPHY

GOTTSCHALK, L. A. and AUERBACH, A. H. (1966), *Methods of Research in Psychotherapy*, New York, Appleton-Century-Crofts.

HALMOS, P. (1965), *The Faith of the Counsellors*, London, Constable.

JACKSON, F. (1973), 'Families and workers in Islington', University of Exeter, B.Phil. thesis published in modified form in *FSU Quarterly*, 5, 1973.

KADUSHIN, A. (1972), *The Social Work Interview*, New York, Columbia University Press.

MCKAY, A., GOLDBERG, E. M. and FRUIN, D. J. (1973), 'Consumers and a Social Services Department', *Social Work Today*, 4, p. 16.

MAYER, J. E. and TIMMS, N. (1970), *The Client Speaks*, London, Routledge & Kegan Paul.

MELTZOFF, J. and KORNREICH, M. (1970), *Research in Psychotherapy*, New York, Atherton Press.

MEYER, H. J. et al. (1965), *Girls at Vocational High*, New York, Russell Sage Foundation.

MULLEN, E. J., DUMPSON, J. R. et al. (1972), *Evaluation of Social Intervention*, San Francisco, Jossey-Bass.

OVERTON, A. (1960), 'Taking help from our clients', *Social Work* (US), 5, pp. 42-50.

PARAD, H. J. (1965), *Crisis Intervention*, New York, Family Service Association of America.

PHILP, A. F. (1963), *Family Failure*, London, Faber & Faber.

PHILP, A. F. and TIMMS, N. (1957), *The Problem of 'the Problem Family'*, London, Family Service Units.

PINKER, R. (1971), *Social Theory and Social Policy*, London, Heinemann.

PLOWMAN, G. (1969), 'What are the outcomes of casework?', *Social Work* (UK), 26, p. 1.

POWERS, E. and WITNER, H. L. (1951), *An Experiment in the Prevention of Delinquency*, New York, Columbia University Press.

REID, W. J. and EPSTEIN, L. (1972), *Task-Centred Casework*, New York, Columbia University Press.

RODGERS, B. N. and STEVENSON, J. (1973), *A New Portrait of Social Work*, London, Heinemann.

ROGERS, C. R. (1951), *Client-Centred Therapy*, Boston, Houghton Mifflin.

ROGERS, C. R. and DYMOND, R. F. (1954), *Psychotherapy and Personality Change*, Chicago University Press.

SPENCER, C. (1970), 'Seebohm, problems and policies', *Social and Economic Administration*, 4, p. 3.

STEPHENS, T. (1945), *Problem Families*, London, Pacifist Service Units.

STREAN, H. (1968), 'Casework with ego-fragmented parents', *Social Casework*, 49, pp. 222-7.

TIMMS, N. (1973), *The Receiving End*, London, Routledge & Kegan Paul.

TRUAX, C. B. (1967), in REID and EPSTEIN.

TRUAX, C. B. and CARKHUFF, R. R. (1967), *Towards Effective Counseling and Psychotherapy*, Chicago, Aldine.

Index

advice-giving, 40, 42, 50, 52, 72-3, 79-81, 84, 87, 92, 131, 159
Assum, A. L. and Levy, S. J., 102
Auerbach, A. H., 93, 94

Bartlett, H. M., 122
befriending *see* caseworkers: friendliness
Berenson, B., 6
Blaine, G. B. and McArthur, C. C., 93
Bott, Elizabeth, 90
Brown, G. E., 101
budgeting *see* financial problems
Butrym, Z., 1

Carkhuff, R., 6, 110; and Berenson, B., 6
caseworkers: authority *see* caseworkers: firmness; changes of, 9-10, 64-5, 68-9, 99-100, 121, 127, 130, 152, 154, 158-9; disclosure of own problems, 53, 72-3, 92, 117, 121, 130, 166; disliked, 35, 50, 67, 77-9, 91-2, 128, 131, 155; empathy with clients, 50, 53, 62, 84-6, 88-9, 91, 105-6, 111, 117, 121, 165-6; firmness, 6, 25, 37, 52, 69, 72-3, 79-85, 88, 91-2, 113, 117, 120, 131, 165; friendliness, 40, 42, 44, 49-56, 58-60, 69, 70, 71-3, 77, 79, 85, 89-90, 92, 104-5, 111, 114-15, 118-20, 130, 151-2, 164; homeliness, 68, 69, 86, 88, 116, 156; influence of sex of, 55; patience, 68-9, 86-90, 106, 116; perception of clients, 4, 18, 31, 38, 94-7, 100-1; professionalism, 38, 42, 49-51, 55, 69, 71-3, 77, 85, 93, 97, 111, 114-15, 117-20; purposefulness, 1-3, 6, 77, 85, 112, 122; student, 50, 66-9, 78, 111, 130, 156; taking trouble, 87, 146, 152, 154
Chance, E., 102
Child Care Service, 122
Child Guidance Service, 144
children: numbers, 10-11, 14, 113; problems and help with, 13, 26, 29, 32, 40, 43, 44, 46, 47-8, 52, 56, 61, 84-5, 95, 108-9, 115, 118, 131-2, 134-7, 142-5, 154, 157
Children's Department, 19, 141, 148, 154, 164
churches, 23
clients: changes during contact, 4, 38-9, 60-1, 94-102, 104, 106-7, 116, 117, 120, 154-5; desire for order, 6; end of contact, 9, 76, 95-7, 99, 100-1, 120, 128, 132, 152, 162; evaluation of caseworkers, 26, 29, 44, 89, 112, 128, 131; expectations of FSU, 4, 9, 17-21, 32, 33, 36, 58, 90, 113, 119, 127, 129, 158, 160; external pressures, 61, 95, 97, 117, 132; honesty with caseworkers, 3, 16, 34, 46-7, 69, 115, 127, 130, 147; identification

171

INDEX

clients—*cont.*
with caseworkers' values, 3, 60, 62, 85, 92, 99, 116-17, 120; inner distress, 13, 61, 95, 97-8, 117, 132; intra-familial performance, 13, 31, 48, 56, 97-8, 101, 104, 122, 136; length of contact, 7, 9, 64-70, 113, 115, 116, 118, 121, 130, 138-40, 156, 166-7; moral evaluations of caseworkers, 5-6, 44, 62, 68, 89-90, 103-4, 106, 110, 116, 121, 146; moral values, 6, 112, 117; own efforts to cope, 21, 25, 112-14, 127, 129; participation in welfare, 72-3, 75-7, 116-17, 150; perception of caseworkers, 8, 10, 17-18, 38, 104; preferences for particular caseworkers, 4, 6, 10, 64-70, 86, 103-4, 113, 116, 127, 130, 152-153, 155, 159, 166; relationships with caseworkers, 10, 34, 47, 71-93, 98-100, 103, 113, 116, 118, 122, 131, 146-7; relationships with other clients, 44-5; role-behaviour, 24, 32-3, 36, 55, 85, 89-91, 119; satisfaction, 17, 28, 30, 32, 36, 60, 62, 92, 97, 114, 116, 121
'closed' families, 7-9, 27, 29-30, 43, 45, 81, 95-7, 99, 101, 118
closure of cases *see* clients: end of contact
clothing, help with, 26, 28, 31, 33, 40-3, 45, 114, 130, 145
Cofer, E. N. and Chance, E., 102
contraception, 40, 52, 134-6
criminal offences, 11, 13-14, 47, 113, 134, 142-4, 146

debts, 11, 13-14, 20, 27-8, 29-30, 46, 49, 57, 81, 113-14, 141, 146, 163; collection to repay, 39-40, 43-4, 46, 56, 59, 75, 80, 84, 148-9
dependence, 35, 51, 53, 55, 67, 79, 93, 119
depression, 20, 27-8, 29, 53, 60, 98, 120, 135, 157-8

despair, 21, 25, 97
discussion, 20, 39, 42, 46-7, 53, 113, 115, 127, 130
Dockar-Drysdale, B., 37
Dumpson, J. R., 1
Dymond, R. F., 102

Education Department, 23, 26, 33, 144-5
Epstein, L., 111
Eysenck, H. J., 101, 110

families *see* clients
family problems *see* clients: intra-familial performance
Family Service Units (FSU): Islington, 92, 145; national survey, 10-14, 27, 113; nature, 3; Sheffield Committee interview, 5, 108-9; style of work, 71, 81, 118, 149; *see also* Unit House
Family Welfare Association (FWA) study, 71
fathers *see* husbands
financial problems and help, 13, 20, 25, 31, 40, 43, 46, 47-8, 56-7, 59, 61, 95, 100, 115, 117, 130-1, 134-7, 167
furniture, help with, 28, 40-3, 114

general practitioners, 19, 23, 157, 160
George, V. and Wilding, P., 18, 36
Goldberg, E. M., 1, 17
Goldring, P., 3
'good' work, 3, 39, 44, 65, 72, 76, 94, 98, 105-11, 113, 117, 122, 132, 147, 149, 152-3
Gottschalk, L. A. and Auerbach, A. H., 93, 94
Grummon, D. L. and John, E. S., 102

Halmos, P., 72
help, 4, 6, 55-60, 112, 114, 116; attitudes to receiving *see* clients: role-behaviour; categories, 39, 71, 113, 130, 152; congruence with

INDEX

help—*cont.*
  needs, 9, 18, 26, 28-9, 32, 36, 58, 97-8, 114, 116, 119, 121, 129; emotional, 28, 30-1, 49, 56, 59, 60, 89-90, 92, 99, 100, 130, 147-153; material *see* material help; non-FSU, 4, 9, 18, 21-4; from relatives and friends, 18, 22, 36, 90, 115, 127, 129, 151
holidays, 40-2, 44, 130
home visits, 4, 34, 46, 55, 114-15, 120
husbands, 4; absent, 11, 16, 21, 22, 26, 27, 57, 64, 136; employment, 10-13, 27, 30, 44, 48, 61, 84, 95-8, 105, 109, 113, 118, 132, 134-7, 152; health and feelings, 46, 134, 136; need to dominate, 55, 115, 120; in prison, 21, 27, 35, 40, 45, 109, 136, 142-3, 164-5; uncooperative, 16, 35, 50, 53, 90-1, 167

interviews, conduct of, 4-6, 14-16, 86, 127-67

Jackson, F., 17, 92
John, E. G., 102

Kadushin, A., 36, 72, 92
Kornreich, M., 111

Levy, S. J., 102
limit-setting, 52, 53, 73, 79-83, 117, 131
loans and grants, 28, 39-40, 42, 56, 59, 80, 114, 146

McArthur, C. C., 93
McKay, A. *et al.*, 1, 36, 62
marital problems, 20, 22, 27, 29-31, 46, 47-8, 53, 54, 55-7, 61, 84-9, 95, 98, 115, 131, 134-7
material help, 20, 28, 29-31, 39-42, 46, 49, 56-60, 68, 70, 91, 114; linked with emotional, 17, 27, 29-31, 43, 93, 114-15, 119; not granted, 26, 28, 42-3, 79-81, 91-2, 100

Maternity and Child Welfare, 19
Mayer, J. E. and Timms, N., 1, 17, 22, 36, 58-9, 69, 71, 93, 111, 121
Meltzoff, J. and Kornreich, M., 111
Mental Health Department, 19
Meyer, H. J. *et al.*, 101
money *see* financial problems
mothers, unsupported, 9, 16, 57-8, 98-9, 118, 120
Mullen, E. J., 1, 101; and Dumpson, J. R., 1

need–help relationship *see* help: congruence with needs
negotiating, help with, 28, 30, 39-40, 43-4, 56, 59, 60, 88, 130, 153

official *see* statutory
'open' families, 7-9, 27, 29-30, 43, 45, 81, 95, 99, 101, 118
Overton, A., 17

Pacifist Service Units, 3
panic, 18, 37, 61, 97-8, 104, 118
Parad, H. J., 101
Philp, A. F., 3; and Timms, N., 3
Pinker, R., 3, 32, 73, 112
play groups, 21, 42, 44, 45
Plowman, G., 94
Powers, E. and Witner, H. L., 101
Probation Service, 19, 21, 35, 142-4, 148, 164

referral: agents, 9, 18-22, 25, 113, 129, 141, 154, 157, 164; by clients, 55, 57, 85, 119, 128, 131, 163; problems at, 4, 9, 11, 18, 20-1, 26-9, 31, 36, 46, 49, 55-7, 95, 99, 101, 113-14, 116, 117, 119, 127, 129, 141-7
Reid, W. J. and Epstein, L., 111
Rodgers, B. N. and Stevenson, J., 123
Rogers, Carl R., 6; and Dymond, R. F., 102

scroungers, 85, 88, 91, 117, 156

173

INDEX

Seebohm Committee, 123
single-parent families *see* mothers, unsupported
Social Security, 24, 35, 145, 148, 153, 160, 162
social services (non-FSU), 21-5, 27, 32-3, 35, 91, 103, 105, 113, 119, 122-3, 127-8, 129, 131, 147, 162; *see also* help, non-FSU; statutory services
Social Services Act, 23
social work: demand for effectiveness, 2, 105, 122; purpose, 1-3, 6, 77, 112, 122
special schooling, 10-11, 14
Spencer, C., 2
statutory services, 3, 24, 32, 87, 105, 117, 122, 150; *see also* Social Security; Supplementary Benefits Commission
Stephens, T., 3
Stevenson, J., 123
Strean, Herbert, 92
'successful' work, 1-3, 36, 39, 44, 70, 72, 76, 93, 94, 98, 105-11, 112, 113, 117, 121-2, 132
suicide attempts, 22, 25, 27, 30, 84, 154, 157, 162
Supplementary Benefits Commission (SBC), 21, 22, 23, 24, 28, 131, 156
support *see* help

Timms, N., 1, 3, 17, 36, 58-9, 69, 71, 93, 111, 121
Truax, C. B., 111; and Carkhuff, R. R., 6, 110

unemployment *see* husbands: employment
'Unit families', 67, 68-9
Unit House, visits to, 22, 45, 55, 67, 114, 127, 160

Wilding, P., 18, 36
Witmer, H. L., 101
wives' health and feelings, 46, 47-9, 98, 109, 115, 120, 134-7; *see also* depression; suicide attempts